This book belongs to:

_____

HOME FROM THE HONEYMOON

The Newlyweds' Guide
to the Celebrations and Challenges
of the First Year of Marriage

SHARON NAYLOR

STEWART, TABORI & CHANG ✦ NEW YORK

Published in 2009 by Stewart, Tabori & Chang
An imprint of Harry N. Abrams, Inc.

Library of Congress Cataloging-in-Publication Data
Naylor, Sharon.
Home from the honeymoon : a complete guide to the celebrations
and challenges of the first year of marriage / Sharon Naylor.
p. cm.
Includes index.
ISBN 978-1-58479-760-9
1. Marriage. 2. Marital conflict. 3. Communication in marriage. I. Title.
HQ734.N375 2009
646.7'8—dc22
2008037917

Editor: Rahel Lerner
Designer: Anna Christian
Production Manager: Tina Cameron

The text of this book was composed in Adobe Jenson.

Printed in the United States of America
10 9 8 7 6 5 4 3 2 1

HNA ▮▮▮▮▮
harry n. abrams, inc.
a subsidiary of La Martinière Groupe
115 West 18th Street
New York, NY 10011
www.hnabooks.com

for Joe

CONTENTS

INTRODUCTION

What are you most looking forward to during your first year of marriage? Waking up every day next to your spouse? Living an idyllic life in your new home? Renovating your home together? Proving wrong all of those dark, cynical reports that say "the first year of marriage is the hardest"? Yes, it's true. Lots of surveys and studies say that the first year of marriage presents a parade of challenges and potential conflicts, even if you've been living together for years. Friends may joke that your sex life will be over, that you should be resigned to a life of nagging and chores. But the first year of marriage doesn't have to be a gauntlet of tests and trials and hard lessons! You can *choose* to make your first year a parade of *celebrations*, focusing instead on the romantic and exciting firsts you'll face together, from the first holiday in your new home to the first Valentine's Day you'll spend together as marrieds, to the first furniture you buy together, to the first time you sign a card together.

It's the couples who don't make an effort to celebrate the exciting firsts of newlywed life who have the most trouble. They're the ones who think only about how tough it can be to split the bills, or who battle over where to spend the holidays. They expect conflict, so that's what they get. Their marriage is a war zone, and the odds are stacked against them.

You'll face these same issues, too, but you now have a guide to turning each emotionally loaded issue—like money and sex—into a fair compromise that becomes easier because your focus is on how lucky you are to have each other. Experiencing each large and small milestone with appreciation and personalization, care and creativity, makes you a better team who can face money, sex, even in-law issues with more of a united front. So celebrating your first-year firsts is foundational as well as great fun. It all works together.

Throughout this book, you'll discover fun and creative ways to celebrate your big firsts and major milestones, plus essential tips from financial experts, family therapists, sex therapists, and other advisors to further help you navigate the land mines you will encounter during your first year of marriage.

Of course, different couples have different styles, different belief systems, and different wishes for their future—such as decisions on having children, name-change options, religious holidays, even when they will take their honeymoon—so while every occasion in the book won't apply to every couple specifically, the techniques and advice shared in each section can go a long way in helping you chart your own course in many situations.

Use this book as inspiration and as a keepsake you'll look back on throughout your lifetime together, so that you can reminisce about your first dinner party, the first holidays you hosted as husband and wife, the first room you painted together, the first time you viewed your wedding video, and more unforgettable moments and memories from this, your first year as husband and wife.

JUST FOR THE GUYS!

Although this book is primarily addressed to brides, creating celebrations and navigating the challenges of the first year of marriage and beyond is always a team effort. So throughout the book, you'll find "Guys' Tips" to help you go from groom to husband, come up with your own surprise ways to celebrate, and steer you away from the most common newlywed-husband mistakes.

PART ONE

Celebrating Your Firsts

CHAPTER 1

Everyday Activities

These are the very first firsts you'll experience as you transition from honeymoon mindset to "we're back in our lives . . . and we're married!" mindset. It's these first celebrations that can be the sweetest of them all.

Your First Night Home from the Honeymoon

Your home is going to look different to you when you return from your honeymoon or from your wedding if you aren't taking your honeymoon until later. Whether you're driving up the street or riding up an elevator to your apartment or condo, there's a whole new meaning to the words "We're home." This might not be your first time in your house as a married couple—maybe you dropped off your wedding gifts after your wedding reception and then headed to the honeymoon suite or the airport—but it is your first time coming home to live as a married couple. The wedding, in all its glory, is over. And now it's the two of you, coming home as husband and wife.

Will you ignore the celebration possibilities here, preferring to just drop your suitcases by the door and collapse on the couch like you've done after every other weekend getaway or vacation? Will you pass through a big Minute One to go check your e-mail or (cringe!) start your laundry?

Don't miss this once in a lifetime first! Here are some ways to make walking through the door an *event*:

* Since this is your first time keying into your home as husband and wife, both of you can turn the key in the lock, then cross the threshold holding hands.
* If he's the chivalrous type, he might want to carry you through the doorway. Forget any notions of whether you *need* to be carried . . . it's just a simple good-luck ritual.
* Hold hands and jump across the threshold together.

Now that you're in, the celebration can continue. Just dump those suitcases to the side for now, and get out your camera. Some celebration shots to get:

* A photo of your still-packed, bulging luggage sitting by the door, especially if you've gotten "Just Married" luggage tags.
* A photo of the two of you holding up the massive collection of mail that has piled up while you were away.
* A photo of your dog welcoming you home.
* A photo of the two of you showing off your tan lines (in a tasteful way, of course).

Depending on what time you get home, you might be ready for another first—your first meal in your home after the honeymoon. Some newlyweds enjoy the wonderful surprise of family and friends filling their refrigerator up with the makings of a gourmet meal, a delicious surprise that has brought some newlyweds to tears over the kindness of their loved ones. They may find a pair of steamed lobsters and shrimp, or a pair of filets mignons, a hearty lasagna cooked by Mom (or Dad), a bottle of champagne or wine, chocolate-covered strawberries, a fresh fruit platter, or other treats. All you'd have to do as newlyweds is change into outfits appropriate for a late-dinner picnic in your living room, or a meal served in bed, and you celebrate this first in an unforgettable way. If your family didn't load the fridge with gourmet snacks and a five-star dinner, there's always the fun of ordering in take-out food. When you're in love, even a lukewarm pizza tastes good!

Another way to celebrate your first night home is to sit down and watch your wedding video. Perhaps your videographer handed over the raw, unedited videotape from your wedding (why pay so much to have it edited now when you can have it done later?) or a relative picked up the edited DVD while you were away. Now, in the quiet of your home and without anyone else's commentary, the two of you can spend your first night at home reliving your wedding day through the footage captured during the blur that was your Big Day. You'll have missed so much while circulating to greet your guests! There's the bridesmaid dancing with the deejay. There are your grandparents dancing to Chris Botti's "When I Fall in Love." There's a shot of your sweetie looking adoringly at you from across the room as you're laughing with your friends. It doesn't get better than this.

If you haven't received your wedding video yet, you can still have a lot of fun checking your e-mail to find those wonderful online photo albums that friends or family have sent to you, filled with the pictures they took on your wedding day. In many instances, these photos are just as high-quality as the professional photographers', and many are funny shots as well. Plus, those who sent you the links will love receiving your thank-you message so soon after you return home from the honeymoon!

If your professional photos have come in, you can flip through them now, but don't try to choose the ones that will be in your wedding album. Now's not the time for work. It's just a time for appreciating your wedding as it happened, and transitioning into your home on this first night together.

The First Time You Wake Up Married in Your Own Bed

Whether it's the sun shining through the window blinds, a neighbor's car horn, or your alarm that wakes you, this is the first and only time you'll wake up for the first time as husband and wife in your own bed, in your own *home*. So don't let this moment get away from you! Don't hop out of bed to race into your day, jump into the shower (alone), or drive off to the gym. Just enjoy being where you are. Enjoy the sound of your spouse breathing peacefully while still in deep sleep. Check out your spouse's eyelashes, his gorgeous profile, or the adorable way his face is smashed into the pillow, or the way his leg is hooked over yours. This is a golden moment, isn't it? Don't disturb it. Don't wake him up because you want to start your day together or go out to breakfast. Just do nothing but listen and enjoy. Sure, you can cuddle in closer and maybe drift back to a blissful slumber yourself. Maybe he'll turn on his side and spoon you in his sleep—is there anything better than that? Maybe he'll sense you awake next to him, reach for you, and start your day off with your first morning wake-up sex. Then you can hit the shower (together) and begin your day however you choose. You've celebrated the moment well, not with party hats and photographs, but with quiet and closeness.

Your First Dinner at Home

You have all of those great wedding gifts—the fine china and crystal stemware, the fondue pot, the stainless-steel saucepan, the stove-top grill, the chef-quality kitchen knives—so now's the time to celebrate the first time you create dinner at home, just the two of you. You both

Our First Dinner at Home

What's on the menu?

_____

_____

_____

Our wine choice:

_____

And for dessert:

_____

might have your favorite recipes—perhaps the very same things you first cooked for each other while you were dating, so what's your first dinner at home going to consist of?

It's incredibly sexy to cook a meal together—the scents of all the spices, the juices of the fruits you're cutting, watching each other's hands work the ingredients. Many newlyweds say they often have to turn off the burners or oven because they find cooking such a turn-on. "That lasagna needs time to cook, so we can go upstairs for a while" gives you time for sex if you're not the kitchen counter or kitchen floor type. Who says you lose your sex life during the first year of marriage? Not those who cook together!

When your food prep time is over, bring out your *Top Chef–* style presentation designs and sauce the plates, present that filet with a mountain of crispy sweet potato fries, serve everything up on the good china, and bring it all to your well-set dining room table to eat by candle-light. Again, this is a first meal at home to be celebrated with five-star attention to detail, the new cloth napkins folded or rolled, and a proper uncorking of your first bottle of champagne or wine together. Keep that cork, too, to add to your collection of special-moment keepsakes.

Even cleanup can be sexy and unforgettable. "You wash, I'll dry," turns into an embrace from behind at the sink, a kiss on the neck, and often a pile of dirty dishes and pans left to soak while you go upstairs for a while. Unless you're the kitchen counter type.

"Go for something cozy in front of a roaring tabletop fire, like fondue, and finish the meal with s'mores using the same Sterno. Anniversaries are the time to pull out all the stops and cook up the recipes you wheedled out of the restaurant where you had your first date. But returning from the honeymoon requires nothing more than a great bottle of champagne and some wonderfully fresh seafood, like oysters."
—Anne Bramley, Cofounder and host of the Eat Feed Podcasts

KEEPSAKE COLLECTION

Label each cork with a note attached to thin picture-hanging wire that you'll insert through the cork itself, then twist to secure. Stickers lose their glue over time, dry up, and fall off, and you don't want to wind up with a box full of dried corks and flaky labels in a mess at the bottom of the box. What should you keep your corks in? You can stash them in a pretty vase (perhaps a wedding gift), a cigar box with a sliding lid, or display them in a shadow box found inexpensively at the craft store.

Hosting Your First Dinner Guests

Okay, you won't be doing anything on the kitchen counter other than preparing the meal for your guests this time around! And again, you can pull out all of those wonderful gifts like your china, crystal, table linens, serving platters, and the like. Turn the preparty cleanup into a celebration, not a stressor. Take an entire weekend day to super clean your apartment or house, turning up your favorite music, maybe ordering in your favorite sandwiches, and compliment the work the other is doing. Even a day spent cleaning together can be great, bonding fun when mixed with the anticipation of your first houseguests. When you're through, a kiss of thanks.

On the night of the dinner, turn on some soft music, light candles, and create a cozy atmosphere that tells your guests "you're special to us, so we did this to greet you." Set a pretty table with your new china and crystal, and add some personal touches to the table, such as place cards and napkin rings that may be family heirlooms. If parents are coming,

Our first dinner guests were:

_____

_____

_____

The meal we served was:

_____

_____

_____

_____

Unforgettable moments included:

_____

_____

_____

_____

they love it when your first dinner includes some of what they've given you, as well. It assures them that they haven't been erased from your lives, and that you love family traditions.

Time your preparations well so that you're not rushing through the food-prep portion of the evening, and make a celebration out of setting the table. This might be the first time you use your new tablecloth, so work together to set it out just right, fold your napkins together, slip on those shiny, new napkin rings. Each step in getting your table ready is a milestone, and it's a wonderful idea to take a picture of your first formally set table.

With the food in the oven, turn your attention to the fun of getting dressed up for your first dinner party. Do you have a classic little black dress and heels? Let your guests know that you're planning to

"Make it simple, make it shared, and make it seasonal. If you had a traditional June wedding, put together easy berries with cream on the menu and shop together for the ingredients at the farmers' market so that you can investigate your new neighborhood together. If you had an autumn ceremony, heat up the kitchen with a rich braised lamb and lovely seasonal apple tartlets made from apples you picked together on a Saturday outing. Be sure to start off with cocktails and end with aperitifs to make the most of all the great glassware you received as gifts. And follow the meal with an offering of local cheeses, which not only celebrates your interest in the place you've made your home together, but also provides an opportunity for all those elegant cheese knives and serving platters to take center stage."
—Anne Bramley, Cofounder and host of the Eat Feed Podcasts

FIRST HUGS WITH FRIENDS AND FAMILY

The return to the normal social world after the wedding can be a bit dicey. Of course, friends and family have raves to share about your wedding, but you want to be careful that social events post-wedding don't continue to focus too much on the wedding. So you have some choices when putting this dinner party together. If you want to make it a thank-you opportunity for family and friends who were part of your wedding, that could be a beautiful tribute, with toasts to the loved ones who got you through the wedding craziness, or little thank-you gifts that you picked up on your honeymoon. They needn't be expensive—a piece of sea glass for the friend who collects the ocean-blue variety, a shot glass for the guy who collects them from all over the world, a packet of bath salts from the spa. You know the items that will tickle your friends and family, and you can make this dinner party a wonderful celebration with a little something that shows you were thinking of them.

On the other hand, if more time has elapsed since the wedding, if you want to invite guests who weren't in the wedding inner circle, or if you fear that you may have been a bit too focused on yourself during the wedding-planning months, now may be the time to have an event that is wedding-free. So you may choose to make this dinner party all about family and friends and food and conversation, leaving out the obvious wedding references. But subtle gestures, like using serving plates that these guests gave you, are always an appropriate and thoughtful way to show appreciation for all that your family and friends have given you.

dress up for this soiree so that they don't show up in jeans and feel underdressed. It's a huge honor to be the first dinner guests, so let them know you're planning something special. Just an e-mail of "We're planning this as a dress-up occasion, so it's time for your little black dress!" takes care of the notification, and guests say they love dress-up dinner parties because they get to impress their dates or spouses, as well. The guys don't have to wear ties. Just make it a no-jeans rule.

One fun aspect of the first dinner party is that you can invite your guests into the kitchen, pour some fantastic wine, and work together on a course. This group-prep party is a popular trend in entertaining at home, since everyone gets to mingle while they're slicing the bread or tossing the salad. Don't make this prep process anything complicated. Even assembling a cheese platter is a fun group effort. And here's the romantic part: Tell the group how much you love your spouse's cooking. We all love it when our partner brags about us, so bring this newlywed must into your home for the first time.

GUYS' TIP

While it may be your bride's friends who extend the most frequent invitations to get together now that you're married, your own friends may want to spend some quality time with the two of you for a relaxing dinner at their place or a night on the town. Perhaps you only got a few minutes with them on the wedding day, so make time for your buddies, and get back to "normal life" after a quick toast to acknowledge your new status as married.

When dinner is served, propose the first toast—and yes, this is the first toast with others that you'll have in your home, so make it count!—and share why it's so special to you that *these* people were the ones you invited. They might be parents, siblings, or members of your bridal party for whom this dinner is another thank you. And with each bite of the meal you enjoy, celebrate the fact that you have such wonderful people in your life. So don't get stressed about overcooked chicken or sticky risotto. Even a dish that comes out badly is to be celebrated . . . it's the first *underwhelming* dish of your first year together. Keep your perspective so that this dinner party is a success no matter what happens.

Enjoy the meal and ask your guests about their lives—it's not all about you and your wedding and your honeymoon. This celebration shows that you've transitioned out of Wedding World, which can be a self-involved place, and you're fully involved in your future as members of this harmonious group of extended family and friends.

After your dinner guests have gone home, share the cleanup duties equally, perhaps even sitting on the kitchen floor together to spoon out the last few mouthfuls of chocolate mousse and feeding them to each other. Dinner hosts get to lick the bowl.

Your First Visit with Family After the Wedding

The last time they saw you was at the wedding. Now that life is on normal mode again, your first visit with your family has a whole new dimension to it. You are now the newly married son or daughter, and your spouse is officially part of the family. That calls for a celebration (unless the reason you're visiting is someone's birthday party or anniversary celebration, in which case you don't want to steal anyone else's thunder by whipping out your wedding album or staging a screening of your wedding video . . . that's just wrong).

If you're in the clear, though, and this is just a family get-together, you can and should share your wedding day images and video with the group. They'll love to go through them with you and share their stories of the things you may have missed while you were off taking your photos and entertaining your guests. How fun for all of you to discover the different views of the wedding day! They may not have known how nervous you were before the ceremony or that your great-grandmother called you that morning to wish you well. Recelebrating the wedding is a key ingredient of this first visit with family. And a fun way to add extra flavor to this event is to bring the family a beautifully decorated cake of their own, something to be cut and served with your parents' wedding knife set if they have one. That's a beautiful way to thank them for all they did for your wedding.

Which brings us to the other key celebration of this day: You're gathering for the first time with your spouse as an official member of the family. So talk with your parents and siblings about how best to "initiate" him or her. You might tell some funny stories about the family's history that he or she has never heard, or get her a mug to match the family nameplate mugs, get him his own Christmas stocking or ornament to match the set the rest of the family has, or some other little tribute to say, "You're one of us now." This is your first family gathering, so pull something from your family traditions to extend a warm welcome to your spouse.

Your First Time Going to Religious Services Together

Religious observance may be an important part of one or both of your lives, so this deeply meaningful first begins a ritual of faith that you'll carry forward into your married life together. Make this first visit to a service something special by dressing up for the occasion, even if your house of worship tends to be a little more casual. Events just seem more special when you put on a dress and he puts on a jacket, and it's far more of a momentous occasion than if you just pulled on a pair of jeans. Dressing up shows respect for where you are.

Perhaps you'd like to thank your spouse in a special way for joining you, especially if he or she is new to the faith thing. Spouses who make an effort to embrace or just understand the other's faith are a tremendous gift, since we all know recently marrieds who tend to give up their former-life traditions to meld into a new unit of matrimony. That's a slippery slope, since you never want to lose *you* in a marriage. When you and your spouse go together, to be welcomed by other parishioners or members of your synagogue community, you gain a sense of belonging that can only support your marriage in the future. So if your religious leader wants to introduce you to the congregation as newlyweds, consider allowing the spotlight to briefly be on you. Take that applause and know that you may be inspiring someone out there who prays for exactly what you have.

Many couples who share a strong faith say that they like to celebrate their first visit to church by stopping to each light a candle at the icons, saying a quick prayer of thanks for the gift of the spouse. Others say they commemorate this first visit to their house of worship by asking their religious leader to bless their rings or their marriage in a quick, informal, and unscheduled manner. This can be a deeply meaningful moment for you both, infusing your marriage with a special blessing said over you, a hand touching your forehead, the smile of a priest or rabbi or minister who radiates joy. Observant couples say this moment is often an ultrapure experience of connection, since they

SHOPPING FOR A CONGREGATION

Some couples shop for a church or synagogue with the best "fit" for them. They want to enjoy the benefits of a regular religious practice in their marriage, and they know you have to find the right place with the right leader, the right tone, and the right message. So a first visit could be the first stop on your search. Together, you'll find the right place where you'll grow and learn and be inspired for many years to come.

may have been nervous during the ceremony and might not have heard what their religious leader was saying. (Many couples watch the video like it's the first time they heard the words.) So if you wish, plan for this very special moment of celebration during your first visit to your chosen house of worship.

Your First Big Dress-up Event

It might be a wedding, a formal party, an office party, a society event . . . it's time to dress to the nines with a formal gown or cocktail dress, a classic tuxedo or smooth suit and tie. It's not every day you both get to dress up like this. The last time you did was probably your wedding day—and don't you just love the way your spouse's face looks when you walk out of the bathroom dressed (or half-dressed) looking like the model makeover version of yourself? He or she may be drooling, which is exactly the effect you're after. So make the *process* of getting dressed part of the "show." Talk with him as you pull up your thigh-high stockings and fasten the garter belt. Ask him to fasten your necklace for you, giving him a great look at your shoulders and the back of your neck. Help him with his tie and run your hands over his arms when you're done with an audible "Mmmmm." Don't put on your shirt just yet. Stop to appreciate your guy bare-chested and in boxers. And since scent is such a powerful part of attraction, spritz on some of your favorite perfume that he loves so much, or ask him to wear that cologne that drives you wild.

Not too many hours from now, you'll arrive back home to make *un*dressing the show. You've read plenty of articles on how to keep the spice in your love life. This is one of the best ways to steam up the start of your married life together. The sight of you, the feel of your dress or stockings, the delicious scent of your perfume . . . this is the stuff passion is made of. And as a first in your marriage, it's priceless!

Your First New Voice Mail Recording

"Hi, you've reached the Andersons!" Nah, too chirpy. "Hi, you've reached the home of Jim and Sally!" Nah, they're reaching your voice mail, not your home. "Hi, we're not in right now." Too clichéd and unsafe if burglars are calling. This first recording of your home voice mail is one of those supersweet tasks. Celebrate not just the recording, but your brainstorming session, too. Bring home some sushi or take-out food, and talk over your ideas for a shared outgoing message. Your first few might be jokes. "We're a little tied up right now" (insert sound effect of whips) "so call us back later" is an example shared by a real-life jokester couple who didn't use that as their final cut. Can one of you do a great celebrity impersonation? Again, maybe too cheesy for you, but imagine the laughs you'll share while dreaming up possible messages. And that's the big word here: laughs. When you can turn a mundane household task into a silly celebration, that's an unforgettable bonding moment, and a first you'll always remember whenever you record a new message or hear some other couple's cheesy voice mail. (That whipped one was much better, you'll recall.)

The First Card You Sign as Husband and Wife

This isn't a big celebration moment requiring champagne and photos, but it is a great little first you can celebrate with a kiss or a hug. The first time you sign your names together is one of those golden moments that you don't want to let slide by unnoticed. Whatever that first card is—a birthday card for a friend, a holiday card, your wedding thank-you notes—you'll both sign your own names in your own handwriting so that you can both enjoy the moment fully. It's just not the same if you write "Love, Anne and Bobby" on your own as you may have done for a long time now. This time, it's different. Now would be a great time to tell your spouse "Even our names look good together!"

Your First Weekend Spent at Home with Nothing to Do

After all of that hectic wedding activity and stress, and catching up on work when you return home from your honeymoon, the first weekend with nothing—nothing!—scheduled can feel very surreal. Do you stay in your pajamas, eat cereal, and watch television all day? You can if that's what you both need, a little time with no to-do lists and no activities, which a lot of couples say is *exactly* what they need since their honeymoon was filled with activities, tours, and island-hopping. They didn't get any downtime there, so they're taking it at home now. If they go back to work on Monday, they want some "lazy time" at home. And that is to be celebrated with cereal served in the good china bowls, ordered-in meals, or comfort food like peanut butter and jelly sandwiches, which can also be served on your choice of bridal shower gifts, such as a platter or appetizer plates.

We spent our first day off:

_____

_____

If you don't want to stay in for "lazy time," you can turn this day into a spontaneous trip, no errands allowed. Is there a fascinating display at the local museum or at an art gallery? What about hopping into the car to take a drive through the countryside. It can be wonderful *not* to have a plan but just go where the road takes you. This style of celebration can become your in-the-moment getaway of choice in the future. How fun to announce, "Let's just go for a drive" and wind up hours later sipping Cabernet at a winery or taking pictures of the fall foliage! You're adventurers together, and you'll be able to celebrate your day of total freedom with a kiss or a toast surrounded by beautiful scenery.

The First Night of TV or Movie Watching

This is one of the firsts that most couples don't realize is a cause for celebration. It might seem like a given that you're going to watch *American Idol* on Wednesday nights, since that's what you always do when the season is on, but now this is your first time watching it as a married couple. The rituals of your engaged days join you in your married days, so the celebration is that *here's something that hasn't changed!* If you're finding yourselves overwhelmed by the amount of change right now (such as moving, combining your finances, name change issues), celebrate the fact that here is something that remains the same. Even the small things like a weekly TV show count, and when you add them up, all of those other changes don't seem like they're the only things going on in your life together. You have to remind yourself to get perspective, so this first night of TV or movie watching can be a very powerful first. If you have a meal you always order in or make during these shows, such as pizza or Chinese food, by all means, stick with your routine. Couples have this great knowledge of what the other likes to eat when they order Chinese food, for instance, so how wonderful a moment is it when he calls to place the order and he knows exactly how you want your General Tso's Chicken?

The first TV show or movie we watched together was:

_____

Even with takeout and even in your pajamas, you can make a celebration out of each commercial break, too. Like three-minute foot rubs or make-out sessions that you can resurrect at your TV-watching rituals long into the future. But you did it first during this first TV night together. The best celebrations become a part of your life going forward.

The First Time You Order Pizza for Delivery

Again, you're taking something you've done a million times in the past and making it a special celebration, just because you can. Your first call to your favorite local pizza place is your first matrimonial order, so get out that fine china, light some candles, set up a picnic on the living room floor, and you'll notice that the pizza tastes even better because you've set an ambiance of celebration. No paper plates for you! And for romance on the sappy side, which could give you a giggle, either feed each other the first bite or entwine your arms to take a bite of your own slice, just like you did with your first sips of wedding-day champagne.

The First Time You Go Food Shopping Together

Now you're taking a mundane errand and turning it into a moment. You've undoubtedly shopped for food together before, but this time is momentous because you're a husband and wife on the task as a team. So grab your shopping list and head out to your local grocery store for that milk, bread, eggs, chicken, and steaks that have become your staples, and then each of you will gather the makings for a special meal you'll cook together this week. This, too, can become a regular practice in your life, making this ho-hum task something special when you know you have his lobster bisque to look forward to.

If your supermarket has those freebie sample displays on the weekends, the mini ravioli, the squares of banana bread, show your love for your partner by getting him a sample, or show your adventurous side by chomping on some never-seen-this-before exotic fruits or imported cheeses. This shopping trip has turned into a little party, with unexpected treats!

The First Seduction at Home Since Your Hot Honeymoon

If there's anything you're going to want to celebrate wildly, it's your first big seduction at home as newlyweds. What's to celebrate besides the obvious? You're "christening" your marriage bed, or your marriage couch, or the stairway if you just look so hot he can't wait until you get upstairs. Some newlyweds make a practice of "Around the World" sex in the home, keeping track of each room or space in the house where they make love, until they "hit" every room. So this first seduction is your takeoff point. Once you choose the place, it's time to choose the lace (bustier, that is) . . .

Lingerie shopping is pure enjoyment, both for you and for him, whether you're in a store looking at see-through corsets, garter belts, and thongs or flipping through a catalog for blush-free shopping at home. Will you choose the outfit, or will he? What's your idea of sexy vs. slutty? This could be the start of your lingerie arsenal, so seduction getup #1 is something to celebrate. Sure, you could pick out something from your existing collection, especially if funds are low after paying for that wedding, and you could revisit something new that you wore on your honeymoon. But for this first seduction? The overwhelming choice is something new. It might be bridal white or electric blue, lipstick red or black with rhinestones—the lingerie you choose then has to be special. Some guys love back-seam stockings

> **GUYS' TIP**
>
> Okay, guys, just because you're married doesn't mean you can get away with wearing old boxers! Ask your bride what she would like you to wear in an upcoming seduction. You may be surprised to find out she *really* wants to see you in boxer-briefs, or even just wrapped in a towel. Married sex doesn't have to get routine, so don't get complacent and do go online to choose a little undersomething to surprise your wife.

for a naughty '50s pinup effect. Visit www.wolford.com for high-end thigh-highs and garters in a range of styles—you're going to need them for your trip around the world in the future. Add in sky-high stilettos, even if you don't make a practice of walking around in them. If you do it right, there's not going to be a lot of walking going on.

Now it's time to set the stage: candles filling the room, rose petals on the bed and on the floor leading up to the bed. New silky sheets in a passionate color. And here's something not everyone thinks of: a love letter on the pillow. Passion needs romance to really sizzle. Your words can light up this seduction.

Is this a planned event, or will one of you surprise the other when he or she comes home from work? "I knew something was going on when I drove up to the house and all the lights were off," says one recent newlywed. "I was hoping that's what it was." Nice. Now here's one word of warning: You don't want your planned seduction to flop, which could happen if your partner is always exhausted when he or she gets home from work. If they regularly sink into the couch and need decompression time, you standing in the doorway in an outfit Bettie Page would envy could potentially fizzle. "Not now," isn't something you want to hear. So make sure this seduction is timed well, suiting your partner's routine.

You don't want to feel rejected as you peel off your own thigh-highs and wipe the red lipstick from your lips while he starts playing video games to unwind. This scenario does happen, unfortunately. So be sure you're not ambushing your partner when you know he's likely to be moody or quiet. Newlyweds need to learn to read their partner's readiness level, which is the number one issue of maintaining a hot sex life.

If all is clear, let the celebration begin. With your choice of music, your grand entrance into the room where he's been asked to wait for you, you're hitting all of his senses.

Again, make sure you know what's sexy vs. slutty, since your seduction can backfire when you pull out the handcuffs or the whipped cream. Not everything you read in magazine articles on "how to keep things spicy" is right for every couple, and you don't want to scare your partner by trying too hard. You know what's on each other's wish list, and this planned celebration is a gift not to be forgotten.

CHAPTER 2

Combining Your Lives

Whether or not you've been living together before marriage, you might already have your finances and policies set in an arrangement that's working just fine for you, and here comes another change! Now you're in a position to get joint accounts, get on each other's insurance since you have signed that marriage license, and handle all the additional paperwork that seals your partnership officially. It can be overwhelming and a little bit scary (*"How are we going to share a checking account?!"*), so just take each task one at a time, consult with professionals to be familiar with the most current laws, and get your papers in order over the first few months of your marriage. In some states, there's a deadline of thirty days to complete a name change and other time-sensitive elements.

Setting Up Joint Checking and Savings Accounts

Before you go to the bank, sit down and decide how you want to divide your accounts. Most financial advisors recommend that couples keep their own checking and savings accounts and then create new shared checking and savings accounts. Filling out the paperwork at the bank should be a snap with the guidance of bank advisors (who will also advise you on handling any name-change issues you have), and soon you'll be dancing at your mailbox when those new checks arrive!

One celebration that newlyweds do when those new checks that bear both of your names arrive is writing themselves a check for a million dollars, or ten million dollars, and stashing it away in a wishes jar or a lockbox. This is one of those dreamy newlywed good-luck charms that gets you to look at your shared finances as a path to your dreams come true, instead of just an obligatory job you'll rush through. These are the

"Simplicity is the key here. You want to have flexibility with a few different account types, but you don't want to make keeping track of your money a chore."
—Jeremy Vohwinkle, Financial Planning Guide at About.com

checks you'll use to secure your future—so writing that fantasy check makes it a special moment. Or mark the occasion with new wallets or checkbook holders.

Keep in mind that it's always a good idea for spouses to keep their own personal checking accounts so that you each remain in control of your own spending, even though you established a new account in both of your names. If you commit to all shared accounts, you may find yourselves drifting into arguments when one of you objects to a purchase made by the other. Separate but equal. A shared account makes you a team, and your individual accounts give you autonomy, which is very important in a good marriage.

Setting Up Your First Joint Credit Card Account

Having good credit is one of the best keys to a happy future and peace of mind, the possibility of buying a home, and even getting good rates on a new car. So adjust your thinking about credit cards if you've always seen them as "free money." They're actually quite important to your marriage, since financial health adds to the health of your relationship.

A joint credit card account needs a big discussion before it is opened. What will you use this credit card for? Improvements to your home? Business expenses for your home office? Just as important as how you'll use your credit cards are the *types* of credit cards you'll acquire. Reward-based credit cards come in many forms; you will certainly find yourselves discussing the benefits of a "cash-back bonus" card vs. an automatic saving card vs. an airline miles card or a rewards account offering gift cards to your favorite stores—or even a credit card offering *several* of these options at once. As a couple, you should discuss the rewards that suit your lifestyle the best (Are airline miles really going to be useful, or would that Target gift card be ideal every two months?). When rewards show up, you'll have to agree on how to share them. You have to spell everything out and agree to the rules you set down. Newlyweds get themselves in trouble when they apply for cards with no agreements up front. That's when impulse spending can become a problem for both of you.

That said, you can turn this first joint credit card account application into a celebration. How fun is it to write down your spouse's name as the second name on the account? Do you have a dream destination for these airline miles? Paris? Italy? The Virgin Islands? Prepare a dish authentic to your dream getaway as a foretaste of what this joint credit card will bring you, or buy a travel book about that special location. This is your first credit card together! As both of you have been responsible with your own credit in the past, so you may also be celebrating your years of smart restraint and good choices, your self-control, your organization and timeliness in paying your bills, your resolve in tough financial times, and the many steps you took in the past to ensure a better future.

When you finish the application, kiss your spouse and talk about the many good things your shared credit will accomplish in the future. And we're not talking about a splurge on a plasma TV or a big vacation you can't afford. Smart use of credit cards is included in the "richer or poorer" section of your vows, so make sure you're investing in being "richer" as best you can.

Changing Your Name

If you choose to change your name, it can feel like more work than the wedding! Especially if this is your second marriage and you have a birth certificate with your maiden name, former married name, and the new married name. You may be running to the Social Security Office and the Department of Motor Vehicles, spending hours at each to get the important task of identity change completed. Add in calls to your credit card companies, bank, and other establishments and you have multiple days of work ahead of you. The good news is that these steps are meant for your security. There's a reason they want to see original documents,

WILL YOU CHANGE YOUR NAME?

One of the biggest identity issues you'll have after the wedding—and perhaps before the big day as well—is weighing the pros and cons of taking your husband's last name. Your family might have strong opinions about tradition, and your friends may be encouraging you to hyphenate your name like they did with theirs. Everyone has a suggestion, and you may be feeling pressure. This is entirely your decision, though. So think about the following: would it hurt your career if you were now known by a different last name? For instance, would all of your published position papers and projects now 'not count' to future employers who find nothing when they Google you using your new last name? What would it take to get your husband's family to understand that your choice not to take his last name isn't an insult to them? Do you like the sound of your potential new last name, or is it an awkward match with your first name? What is your deepest feeling about hyphenating your name with your husband's? These may be tough questions to ask, but they'll lead you to make your own best choice without outside influence. You might decide to change your name legally to his, but create your own transition by working under your first name, maiden name and married last name for a few months as you complete the name-change task. Future employers will then be able to 'connect the dots' from your prior identity to your new one, and you may be more comfortable with easing into the new last name this way, too.

so that takes the sting out of having to track down your birth certificate and other papers. This is all for your benefit, and it completes the process of becoming a Mrs.

While you're in the middle of name-change hell, make sure you're keeping an organized list of where you need to make the switch, and celebrate each one as it's completed. "Today, my credit cards have all been switched to my new name!" deserves a cupcake. Those hours on the phone with customer service earned you a treat, after all. Those three hours at the DMV have definitely earned you a lunch out at your favorite restaurant or a half-hour massage at the gym.

If you're feeling a strange sense of sadness right now, don't be alarmed. This is a big transition, and letting go of your former last name may bring with it a sense of mourning. Happens to so many women—unless they really disliked their last name.

This is a big job, but just like the wedding, once you get into it, it flows.

GUYS' TIP

You are probably just looking on as your wife wades through mountains of paperwork and has a mile-long to-do list to get her name changed, so your support and celebration are essential. So greet your frazzled wife with flowers and a foot rub, and enjoy the complete name change with her first monogrammed personal note cards, a spa robe with her new initials, new name and address mail labels, or a love note addressed to her with her new name. (It's official! Her driver's license says so!)

Creating a Budget

No one really enjoys setting up a budget, nor sticking to one. It can feel like you're dominated by numbers on a piece of paper. No, it's not fun having to "obey" a written budget and it's definitely not fun being the

Building Your Starter Budget

1. List your fixed expenses:

Rent / mortgage _____

Car payments _____

Groceries _____

Internet charges _____

Cell phone _____

Cable bill _____

Gym membership _____

Insurance payments _____

Other: _____ _____

Subtotal _____

2. List essentials that vary:

Utilities _____

Car maintenance and fuel _____

Dining out _____

Phone bill _____

Pet expenses _____

Medical bills _____

Prescriptions _____

Clothing _____

Other: _____ _____

Subtotal _____

3. List leisure expenses:

Movies   _____

Nights out   _____

Coffee   _____

Books and magazines   _____

Attending weddings and parties   _____

Music purchases   _____

Other: _____   _____

Subtotal   _____

Total   _____

Over time, try to trim down the leisure expenses, and get creative on finding new ways to save money. When you "defeat" a new category in your budget—such as dropping the gym membership you never use and working out at home—you and your spouse can celebrate this budget victory with an actual victory lap around the track or the block.

"Marriage presents a unique opportunity when it comes to insurance. If each person in the relationship has a job with benefits, you'll have a decision to make regarding who supplies the coverage. Insurance plans offered by employers vary greatly, so it is important to go over the details of each plan to ensure you are able to find appropriate coverage at the best price. While health insurance is important, newlyweds also need to seriously consider life insurance. You want to make sure that if something unexpected happens to one of you, the survivor will have sufficient financial resources going forward."

—Jeremy Vohwinkle, Financial Planning Guide at About.com

spouse who is establishing this smart-money management plan. What *is* fun? Reaching that point where budgeting $300 a week for groceries comes naturally and neither of you impulse-shop because you know the cable bill is due soon—or because you agree that saving money to buy a house is an important goal. A budget teaches you to divvy up your money for the benefit of your family.

How do you establish a budget? Begin with a Starter Plan—a first attempt at creating a workable budget. If your computer has Quicken or Microsoft Money software, you already own a fantastic tool to help you create and manage your budget. These programs list the top categories of your expenses, such as mortgage or rent, groceries, insurance, utilities, and the types of expenses you incur for entertainment and clothing. You record each of your payments, right down to your morning Starbucks fix and those tickets to a minor-league baseball game with the guys. Click on a button and the program shows you your Starter Budget or an itemized list of what you're spending. This is often a jaw-dropper, since many couples see for the first time that they spend a fortune on clothes and dinners out and their cell phone plans. Changes must be made! That's where step two of your making a budget milestone comes in. Either on paper or with financial software, create the first draft of your Starter Budget with your *fixed* expenses written in, then the limits you'll impose on entertainment, clothing, coffee, etc., so that your weekly and monthly tallies fit well with your income, *and* you have extra to pay off any credit card bills, student loans, and the wedding, and put some money into savings. When a healthy budget is reached, celebrate this important document with some luscious, green healthy salad or a warmed-up whole-grain baguette. Grains are a symbol of abundance, so even a whole-wheat pizza is a celebration with symbolism. Agree to be flexible when you find that your guesstimate of $200 a week just isn't enough for groceries. Meet again to rework the budget, shift another $100 into groceries, and shave $100 off your home décor column. Those new curtains can wait. No splurge is a celebration if it's off the budget!

If you're not accustomed to living with a budget, you might both meet it with resistance, and in the first few months of marriage probably ignore it altogether. But when bills start coming in, you'll be sticker-shocked into reaching for that Starter Budget as a guideline to better controlling your spending.

Keep in mind: This budget is just to keep you in line. It's not a law, so don't force-feed it to your spouse. If it's limiting some parts of your spending, it's doing its job. Over time, you'll both grow to accept and follow your budget automatically, knowing that groceries are in the $300 zone every time you shop. You'll ultimately be in a position to celebrate, knowing that you *own* your financial plan, you've both cocreated a workable, flexible spending program that keeps you in line but doesn't make you feel deprived. That's great work in a healthy marriage!

Setting Up Insurance Policies

You have to protect your health, your home, your money, and your spouse in case the unforeseen comes to pass, so that means setting up new insurance policies to include both of you, or setting up your first life insurance policy. This may involve a mountain of paperwork for each policy you need, the hassles of red tape with your health insurance company, and long stretches of time spent on the phone with agents. For instance, if you decide to get on your husband's health insurance, you may have to cancel your plan, get on a COBRA plan for the interim, and then fill out the necessary paperwork to get yourself on his plan. It's a lot of work that you'll tackle together, though you should consult with an expert when it comes to life insurance plans and home insurance, and consider multiple policies with one company (such as home and car insurance in one group). With insurance being so important, you don't want to take chances by going it alone, so do invest in good advice. Relatives and friends are often a great source of referrals. You should ask who they have their house insurance with.

You're back in the same zone as you were with your wedding plans—comparing packages and rates, learning all you can about what serves you best, and celebrating each task as you complete it. And when your new policy arrives in the mail, know that you are protected. You're doing the smart work of combining your lives with safety and security in mind, and the relief you'll feel at this important milestone is a well-earned celebration.

Creating Your Wills

No one is too young to have a will. No matter what you own, you need to create legal documents naming your spouse as your beneficiary, providing for your kids or parents if you wish, fulfilling all the legal requirements so that matters can be handled in the event of an accident or sudden illness that takes your life. Mortality might not be on your radar right now, but you'd be surprised how many young couples find themselves faced with tragedy, and the surviving spouse is left with bureaucratic nightmares because there was no will.

Visit an attorney for expert guidance on your wills, living wills, medical directives, and other documents that are a part of your "for better or for worse" vows. Making a will is a gift to your spouse. It says, "I love you enough to protect you if anything ever happens to me."

What about will-making software? These programs may be valid in some states, but your best move is to meet with a trusted attorney who can help you draw up the real deal, bringing in every current state law, covering you for death taxes and other statutes. There's an entire branch of legal experts who just do wills and family legal paperwork, so depend on the pros who get regular updates on the issues that will affect your paperwork. This is no time to cheap out.

How do you celebrate *this*? Try a time of intimacy, such as cuddling together, breathing in each other's scents, and absorbing how much you each love having your spouse right there by your side, safe and healthy.

Creating Your Housework Division Plan

Again, it can be a challenge to make a celebration out of sitting down to hash out who's going to do the laundry, and the dishes, and who will pick up after the dog, but you can remove the manual-labor aspect of your list and focus instead on the bigger meaning of "we're creating the plan for *our* home." You're not just doing the dishes, you're coauthoring the mechanics of keeping a comfortable, clean, and relaxing home atmosphere. So *that's* what you're celebrating here, by pairing this sit-down talk with a fabulous home-cooked meal (made in your clean kitchen), and the promise of sharing a delectable dessert after you're done.

How do you announce this sit-down best? Make sure you're honoring your partner's circadian rhythm. If postwork is a recharging time for either of you, it would be counterproductive to expect a detailed talk about toilet cleaning duty. Instead, set the stage for success by saying, "When do you have five minutes to talk about how we'll divide up chores? I made a lasagna and some chocolate mousse that we can have to celebrate getting this mapped out." You've dropped your reward, so that may be enough of an incentive. Don't be surprised if it doesn't happen today. If your partner's mind is jammed with work issues, there are just not enough neurons firing to allow for a new task like this. Allow for a future date to be planned so that you don't set the stage for disaster. When you do sit down to chat, there's a starter checklist on the right to make it go smoothly, and thus let the celebration begin sooner.

You get to create your own list, which might include watering the plants or cleaning the fishbowl. Now here's the best part: You get to choose to be flexible. If someone is starting to hate his or her task, you switch. You should state that now. Everyone loves having the "out," knowing they're not locked into a lifetime of changing the bedding. Stating this makes you a great partner, not a dictator! Or, you might decide together that it's time to hire a housecleaner or a landscaper. The first year of marriage is entirely a learning experience, full of trial and error, learning each other's style. And whenever you're learning each other's ways, you're going to hit some land mines. See pages 177–179 for how to handle your first conflict over who does which housework.

How else can you celebrate completing this essential lifestyle task? Think about some fun theme gifts, such as a cute apron with his name on it for those meals he'll be making, a gift card to Home Depot for the lawn-care tools you will need, a new cookbook, a gift card for a manicure to rescue your nails from dishpan or gardening damage, and, of course, a great thank-you note for being such a great partner and caring about your home. Gratitude is the golden key to a successful first year of marriage. Never forget that.

Your Starter Household Task List

Task	His Job	Her Job	Shared Job
Food shopping	○	○	○
Dusting	○	○	○
Vacuuming	○	○	○
Taking out the trash	○	○	○
Bundling the recycling	○	○	○
Taking out the recycling	○	○	○
Cleaning the bathroom	○	○	○
Raking the leaves	○	○	○
Mowing the lawn	○	○	○
Weeding	○	○	○
Doing the laundry	○	○	○
Changing the bed linens	○	○	○
Doing the dishes	○	○	○
Emptying the dishwasher	○	○	○
Weekly meal prep	○	○	○

Creating Your Home Maintenance Plan

This is your plan for the big things: any plumbing issues that arise ("we'll call a pro, no matter what") or electrical work ("my Dad can teach me how to install new light fixtures this weekend"), future expensive replacements like the air conditioner or boiler ("three years from now, according to the maintenance records"), an addition to your house ("when the baby arrives"). This discussion can become a Dreaming About the Future chat with a little bit of *whew!* built in, relief that you won't have to face a major remodeling for a few years. You'll be surprised how much tension melts away for new home owners when you prethink these big home requirements. So turn this task into a celebration of setting down your future goals onto paper. Be grateful that you have such a great partner with whom you'll face these issues when they arise and pat yourselves on the back for having the foresight to plan ahead.

Creating a Plan for Your Children

In the business of planning your life together, one of the big questions that will come up is "Are we going to have kids?" If the answer is "yes," when you're both in the mood to dream about the blessings of the future, you may mix the realistic (such as when your finances will allow) with the fanciful (what you'll name your babies), and probably tell your spouse "I hope he has your eyes" or "I hope she has your generous nature" as the hallmarks of newlyweds' sweet words to one another. For now, put the pressures of expectation aside and just paint some pictures of how great a parent the other will be someday, how you'd like to raise your children, express your wishes about future family vacations to Disney World, how you can't wait to buy little pink dresses, and how much you love watching your spouse play with the nieces and nephews. These *words* are the celebration. Your spouse will never forget your expressions of how highly you think of him or her, your vote of confidence, and that sets the stage for later chats about "should we start trying now?" You've shared your belief in your partner's parenting skills, and maybe some fears about parenting in general. You're opening up in a dazzling display of intimacy and trust and sighing over the "someday" that you hope to share when the time is right.

Now if you already have children between you, or from previous relationships, this chat might be more business-based, such as how you'll handle their college funds or where to send them for summer camp or when you'll fix up an extra room in the house to give your preteen her own room. As parents, this conversation is all-important, since it sets the groundwork for the business of raising your kids together, and again those words of confidence in your partner and plans for the future become the celebration and the gift.

The names we like for our children are:

_____

_____

You'll have few more important talks in your life, so this first is a momentous one. Record your decisions and visions in a journal as a keepsake for the future. Someday you'll smile about your early thoughts about planning for your family's future.

Putting Your Names on the Mailbox

It's a huge symbolic moment to mark your mailbox or apartment mail slot with both of your names, if living together is a new thing for you or if you've just moved into a new place. You're saying *this is our home*. And that's really an important first if one of you has moved into the house or apartment previously inhabited by the other. There's no *yours* or *mine*. It's *ours*, as proven by the names on the mailbox. So make it a moment.

If you're in an apartment, your mail slot may have room for a tiny slip of paper displaying your last name only, so make it a celebration when you remove the old slip and insert the new one you printed up. You both live here now! It's official! Now how will you celebrate? One shared celebration is doing a little online shopping to buy your new return address labels, stationery imprinted with your names and address, and other newly monogrammed items that give you the thrill of your new identity. These can be a gift from one of you to the other, and, at this point in your life, it's incredibly exciting when you are addressed as a couple. And think about mailing your spouse a love note or stashing a little gift in the mailbox for him or her to find. What a great celebration when there's a love note or gift from you mixed in with those bills and catalogs!

The First Time You Go Car Shopping

Perhaps for the first time, you have to think function before form when buying a car together. Does your new lifestyle, including working on your home, mean that you'll need a roomier trunk than a sports car would provide? "I feel like such an adult!" says one recent newlywed who bypassed the hot little two-seater for a more spacious car. Indeed, looking together at minivans means you've grown up, so instead of mourning your lost youth, turn this into a celebration with lunch after your walk through the car lot, or dinner after your test-drive. And on the day of your purchase, your celebration might mean getting that mug or hat with the car company's logo, new car mats from an auto supply store, personalized plates, or a GPS system to deck out the "new baby."

Talk about what these new wheels are going to allow you to do. Maybe you can stop borrowing your brother's truck when you have to bring big items home. Maybe you can make a plan for a top-down drive in your new convertible through the town or countryside. Maybe you're just happy that your spouse has a safer ride now that he's ditching the car with the shot struts. If you've been driving out to pick him up when his old car has broken down every other week, celebrate the freedom this new ride provides. A car is more than just transportation, it's possibility. It may be a ticket to expand your world, now that you have a new car to drive long distances for a weekend away, or use its four-wheel drive to get up to the mountains for a ski retreat. Where would you like to drive off together as your first minigetaway in your new ride?

Celebrating the new car you share means celebrating the way your entire future changes—for the better.

Changing Your Status on Forms for Work, Clubs, Doctors, etc.

This is more of a little personal thrill than cause for a five-course dinner out on the town, but it is wonderful to celebrate "making it official" in the sense of filling in your spouse's name on work forms, and as your "in case of emergency" person on your medical records. Newlyweds say they love getting that phone call from their spouse at work, saying they just filled in their name on official paperwork. Isn't it amazing how a very small change can feel like a very big deal?

Speaking of big deals, this is also the time that your spouse may be allowed to be added to your club memberships, such as frequent shopper cards, health clubs, town pools, country clubs . . . and you get added to theirs. Each one is a celebration of how fully your lives are combining and the family unit you are. Even if you can just get into Costco on his membership card now,

The perks of our combined lives are:

_____

_____

_____

_____

_____

that's a fun little plus! What are the perks of your combined lives?

Celebrate your spouse's official "welcome to the club" by planning a day at that beach club, and see him beam when he's allowed into the VIP suite with you or when the cabana attendant already knows his favorite drink (if you planned ahead and tipped the attendant off before you both arrived). The day made possible by your partnership is your reward.

If the change was made to any form where "marital status" is the issue, celebrate the milestone with a feel-good thank-you e-mail or text message to your spouse: "Thank you for marrying me. I just checked 'married' for the first time! And I love being married to you!" are sweet rewards to your spouse—and a great way to celebrate.

A fun gift idea: Since you "checked the box" with your new status, get a little gift for your spouse, place it in a little white gift box, and draw a big "check" on the top and sides of the box. What's inside? You get to choose!

CHAPTER 3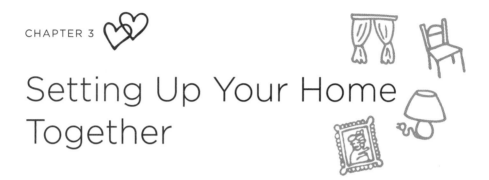

Setting Up Your Home Together

Your marriage is centered in your home, so now's the time to celebrate either establishing your shared home for the first time, or getting to decorate, redesign, or remodel your shared home! You've watched so many home décor shows with interest (and perhaps a touch of envy!), and you finally get to look at paint chips, assess your land-scaping needs, and build your dream home step-by-step using wedding gifts and your first free time since you got engaged. Get ready to have some fun!

The First Major Piece of Furniture You Buy Together

It might seem like just a purchase made out of necessity—a new bed, a new couch, a dining room set—but you can turn this big-money purchase into a celebration when the truck pulls up in front of your place and the movers haul in your beautiful mahogany headboard, or that luxurious sectional with the ottoman and recliner! No matter whose credit card this particular purchase went on, this is your *first* major purchase for your home!

You don't need to call in a religious officiant to say a blessing, but you can create your own way of welcoming in all the new pieces of furniture you buy together. Take a moment to appreciate each one, and share a vision of how you'll use it together in the future. And then, for couches and beds, chairs and recliners, cuddle up in it together and watch a movie or just enjoy some quiet time listening to each other breathe or reminiscing about the shopping trip itself: "I'm so glad we got the king-size! It reminds me of that great night's sleep we had at your family reunion in Vermont." *That* is the best way to celebrate a new furniture buy.

The First Major Appliance You Buy Together

When asked about their first major appliance purchased together, newly-weds beam about their stainless-steel refrigerators right out of the pages of upscale decorating magazines, the fact that they will never have to wash dishes by hand again now that they have an energy-efficient dishwasher, and their new freedom from coin-operated washing machines. A new appliance means a liberated lifestyle, separating you from the perils of your early apartment and college dorm days. "I'm in my thirties. It's about time I owned a washing machine," says one newlywed, who actually popped open a champagne bottle to celebrate with her husband when the installers hooked up their new front-loading washer-and-dryer set. No more quarters! To celebrate further, they took their old quarter collections, brought them to the bank, and transferred them into dollars—enough for a nice dinner out on the town.

When you're in a new home, the sounds of these new appliances make for beautiful music to your ears, and we know of many couples who jump up and down like little kids when that dishwasher finishes its first cycle. It's a beautiful moment, the celebration of having an automated assistant in the kitchen who will free you up to do other things after dinner. And maybe your new microwave sends you into a wave of bliss now that your popcorn will no longer be burnt at the bottom of the bag. Movie night will never be the same.

The first appliance we bought together was:

_____

_____

We celebrated it by:

_____

_____

_____

Deciding Whose Stuff to Use

If you had not been living together before the wedding, the first few weeks after the wedding will find you adjusting to your new shared home and blending everything in it. The shower and wedding gifts have all been put into play, with those plush, fluffy towels in your bathrooms, your stainless-steel cookware in the kitchen, the china in the china cabinet, and the blender on the counter. It's unbelievably thrilling to set out all of the shared items in your home, and then approach phase two of your house blending: deciding whose stuff you're going to use from the *His* and *Hers* collections of your prior lives.

Now here's where you can leap over a land mine: Don't turn this into a territorial issue, or get greedy about wanting more of your things than his in the house. A loving newlywed doesn't try to erase the other or control the style of the home. You're not in a competition to see who can get more of their own things into the kitchen drawers—that's the wrong way to approach blending your lives. That's a kids-in-the-sand-box mentality; aggression about possessions. You're above that.

So turn this into a party! Go through your things and cheer for the fact that you'll be using his way-better-than-yours microwave. Dance around a little bit when you hang your pictures on the walls, finding the perfect places for his ocean prints *and* your floral prints. Kiss each other for every compromise, and top off the party with the promise that you can make changes in the future. Don't toss the other's stuff right away. It'll all go in the attic or storage space for now. Six months down the road, you can decide where to donate it. That takes the "I've been replaced" terror out of blending a home, allowing you to fit the pieces of your lives together like a gorgeous new puzzle. Frames can be changed out, slipcovers can go over that old sofa he loves for its cushiness, and adjustments can be made to merge your stuff. That, too, is something to celebrate with a great lunch ordered in while you're working together. Which take-out menu is your favorite? Ordering your "usual" is a great way to add balance to your possessions-combining milestone. Each of you order and share.

And those things of his that you love? The shining espresso maker? The grandfather clock? The Escher prints? They become a part of *your* home, as do all the things you bring to the table (or the kitchen or the bedroom). So celebrate each item placement, each arrangement of books on a shelf, even if he wants them laying flat and you want them upright. Split the difference, half vertical and half horizontal, and then celebrate *that*. You're both the artists of your home.

Your First Garage Sale Together

Okay, it's been six months and those old pressboard shelves are never going to be used. The light-wood shoe racks that don't go with the new hanging shoe organizers you bought together using wedding shower gift cards? They can go into the garage sale collection, too.

This is an amazing moment in your home creation: You're clearing out the old, the outgrown, the unstylish, the unwanted gifts, the books you've read, the old CDs, your previous mismatched collections of utensils, and a few hundred plastic hangers, the relics of your single lives and the things that have been replaced by your spouse's things or by wedding gifts. You're clearing out space in your home, directing items to people who can use them, and shedding clutter together. How symbolic! It's a new world you've created and some of your things just don't fit in anymore.

How is it possible to celebrate a garage sale? Aren't you just sitting out in the sun for hours on end, getting way too excited every time a car pulls up in front of your house, suffering the insults of people who try to bargain you down even further? Yes, and that's exactly why it needs a celebration element. Each sale gets a high-five or a hug between the two of you, lunch can be from your favorite deli, or you can have a lemonade toast, apply sunscreen to each other's faces, make fanciful plans for the $12 you've earned so far this afternoon, share stories about the items in your garage sale (like that prom dress or your impressive childhood collection of Smurfs that you're finally willing to part with now) for even sweeter insights into your younger days or family memories. You'll share laughs and fun stories from your past, impress him with your defenses against the Angry Bargain Hunter, and show your benevolence when you let the struggling single mom with the five kids in tow take all of those Smurfs away for free.

And even if you make no more than that $12 all weekend, which might happen, that could be the first deposit into your second honeymoon account.

Your First Home Décor Discussion

Your stuff may still be in boxes, and you may have lots of white walls to paint. Now's the time for a celebration of your blank canvas, which you get to paint your own colors. This celebration might take place in the paint sample aisle of Home Depot or your local hardware store, with a wall of beautiful hues in front of you, or you might start the celebration by flipping through some decorating magazines or Pottery Barn catalogs at home. Browsing through magazines while in bed is a fantastic idea— it's the perfect place for dreaming about your home. Cuddle and share your vision: "I see a big oak armoire over there, and an ottoman in front of the fireplace . . . And what do you think about a persimmon color for the second bedroom instead of pink? . . . I think it's much richer and warmer, don't you?" The actual prices of that armoire and the ottoman don't come into play yet, so the dreaming and the visions you trust each other enough to share are the true celebration.

Some newlyweds say they fall in love all over again when their spouses talk about how that second bedroom could be the nursery someday, "so we should paint it sage green now."

"When it comes to the major pieces of furniture and selecting a color scheme for a room, there should always be open dialogue between partners. Color is a very healing force and a personal decision. Fortunately in [my] marriage, we both respond to similar palettes. As a designer, naturally, my husband trusts my instincts and responds to my design aesthetic, but I still always ask his opinion on all things, as I want him to feel inspired by his surroundings."

—Kim Parker, Author of *Kim Parker Home*

Celebrate this chat by putting those paint color sample strips, those torn-out pages from the furniture catalog, and your notes or sketches into a colorful folder or binder as keepsakes of this chat. You'll add to the collection later, and you may pull out that lime green paint strip and laugh. "What were we thinking?" Establishing this Dreams Folder shows that the future is a priority to you both, that you value each other's ideas enough to save them, and you love your home enough to make it beautiful.

Your First Painting Party or Home Project Together

Now *this* is a celebration! You've chosen your colors for the room, bought paintbrushes and drop cloths, and you're ready to roll. Forget about inviting friends over to make the job go more quickly this time around—this one is just for the two of you. So grab your camera, since there are so many big moments in this first. Get a "before" photo of the room, then snap it again when you have all the windows taped off. Take pictures of each other holding your paintbrushes and get a shot of the very first stroke of color that you put on the wall. Again, years later, when you've been living in that gorgeous blue-walled room, you'll gasp at the "before" shots of the white walls. How fun is it to see you painting together for the first time, especially knowing you had the presence of mind about the future to capture that first streak of color.

Turn on some great music and shake it a little while you're painting those walls. You can be a flirt while you work. Every now and then, take a glance over at your spouse up on that ladder painting the upper edges, and tell him how awesome his arms look right now. And no, the fumes haven't gone to your head. He really *is* that sexy. And if you're not painting, but are putting down floor tiles or working on some other big project, make it the same celebration, complete with music, photos, and lots of compliments.

And when you're done, take your "after" photos of the room for your album—your project just might be ideal for one of those home makeover competitions, so if you happen to win $25,000, *that* could be something else to celebrate. Money aside, what you're cheering about right now is that you've just completed a momentous task together, as husband and wife, covered in paint flecks or wallpaper glue, arms aching from a job well done, together!

Cheers to many happy moments in that room.

Your First Shopping Trip with Your Wedding Money or Gift Cards

It's the "kid in a candy store" analogy, as the two of you grab your pile of gift cards, or pull out that envelope stuffed with cash, for a guilt-free shopping trip, possibly at the store where you have registered. This is your most celebrated shopping spree, since you're funded by the love and generosity of your wedding or shower guests. By giving you gift cards or cash, they've also given you an even more valuable experience: getting to pick out *anything you want*. What could be more fun than that?

Maybe you didn't get some essentials, like bath towels or a toaster, so they're on your list, and maybe you never dreamed you'd be able to afford that $300 luxury bedding set or that high-end luggage set. But they're yours to pull off the shelf now, and you'll be giddy with a second wave of "aren't we lucky?!" Imagine yourselves as the recent bride and groom pushing *two* shopping carts overflowing with beautiful things, and each stop in each section of the store opens up new possibilities: "I'm going to get this waterfall showerhead for you!" and "I'm going to get you this top-of-the-line coffee grinder!" This allows you to gift each other with the money you've already received, and these choices are among the best ways to celebrate your shopping spree. It shows you're thinking of the other's happiness and indulging them for everyday life in the future.

Now here's another perk: Many stores with registries offer completion programs that give newlyweds an extra 10% to 15% off the items that remain on their registries. That could stretch out your gift card tally tremendously. Getting an extra 15% off that bedding set? Sweet! That leaves you with money for barbecue grill baskets or fondue plates!

At the end of your "free" shopping spree, you'll probably be tired from the extended excitement and perhaps the heft of all those packages, so continue the celebration after you wrap up at the cash register owing *nothing* (or *almost* nothing) by going to a nearby restaurant for drinks, lunch, or dinner to toast your amazing shopping day. You've made great choices—starting with marrying each other—so you deserve that margarita or that platter of quesadillas as your reward and celebratory meal. Your loved ones have given you a once-in-a-lifetime dream shopping day, so that's definitely something you'll remember always.

Your First Decision on Your Personal Spaces

Virginia Woolf famously wrote about every woman needing "a room of one's own," and just about every design show on television has spotlighted a "man cave" or "the guy room" denoting separate rooms or spaces for the husband and wife in the home. As much as you love each other and as fully as you're blending your lives, it's a wise and wonderful idea to establish and celebrate your own *His* and *Hers* spaces. The size and scope of them are up to you. Some newlywed wives claim a second bedroom as their own room to decorate, where they read or write, and some claim a single comfy chair in the living room for the same purposes. That corner, with her Victorian light stand and floral pillows on the cushy chair, is *Her* space. Some newlywed men claim the garage, or a basement den for all of the hunting gear or movie posters that don't work anywhere else in the house, plus a television and DVD player or game room equipment. These personal spaces are sacrosanct, with the "owner" making all aesthetic decisions and maintaining it on their own.

"I still have my space, my books, my leather recliner. I haven't gotten 'erased' from my own house by all-new furniture and Tuscan motif fabrics throughout the house," says one new husband. Where's the celebration? Primarily, it's a feeling of being respected and *not* being controlled by your partner, and welcomed to make your own decisions in nesting a way that makes you happiest. The secondary celebration is sharing the completion of each room or area as a couple. So when the last book is placed on the shelf, the last Bud Light sign installed over the bar in the basement, cheer your personal spaces with an impromptu party, photographs, lots of compliments (and *no* critiques or "I'm just trying to help" suggestions). You can also pick up a gift for the room. It might be an item you know she saw in a store and loved, such as an antique hatbox or a frame for photographs. Or it might be a gift card to a decorating center so that your partner can go on another guilt-free shopping spree to indulge in some new items for his or her space. Might these rooms join your "Around the World" plans sometime soon?

The First Time You Pay the Mortgage or Rent Together

Few people celebrate writing a big, giant check, but this one is quite special if it's your first shared mortgage or rent payment. This makes you true, equal partners in your home, and some newlyweds say it's the first time they feel like "real grown-ups." So rather than trudging toward your checkbooks, make this an *experience*. Sit down to a home-cooked dinner, pour glasses of wine, turn on some moment-appropriate music (Do you know of any songs with an "our house" theme? Crank them up!), and send payment #1 out into the world as you enjoy the home life that your mortgage or rent agreement allows you to enjoy. This way, that big chunk of money isn't a burden, but a blessing! You have to reframe the meaning of it, thinking and talking about all the things this home allows you to do. And that's worth every penny.

The First Discussion You Have About Moving to a New Place

If you're cramped in a one-bedroom apartment, or if a job prospect could send you to a warmer climate or exciting metropolitan area, the topic of putting down new roots somewhere may arise right now. While we all get a little bit nervous about change, or the prospect of moving far from family and friends, this possible move likely has far more advantages to it. Imagine living in another state where things are far less expensive, where you could easily buy a three-bedroom house. Imagine having no commute, or living in a vibrant city full of cultural hot spots and great restaurants. Your married life will get a whole new vibe. This first chat about moving to a new place centers on your creative imaginings of how wonderful a move could be, if you choose to make it so. What a downer it would be to start moaning about the stress and work of packing—that just closes you off to new possibilities.

So kick off your first move discussion with some fun Internet surfing on real estate and tourism sites to pick out the neighborhoods you would like to consider. You may find that prices are way lower than you expected, or that a particular condo development in Chicago has a pool, a movie theater, on-site dry cleaning, and a gym right in the building. This search can get you dreaming and imagining a life that could be a great relief from the overcrowded situation you're in now. No need to send for change of address forms now . . . the work of the move isn't upon you yet. This is just your celebration of an adventure awaiting you, when you start that wonderful conversation of sharing the places you've always wanted to live and why. And many newlyweds say their spouse's positive attitude and enthusiasm takes the pressure off of them when it's a job transfer or a new business opportunity they'd been concerned would upset their spouses. If you turn this into a celebration, that's a loving gift of relief to your partner.

The First Time You Go House- or Apartment-Hunting Together

Even the bad ones can be fun. Your realtor has asked what you like, and soon you're on the evening tours of local homes, condos, or apartments for rent or for sale. Couples cruise the multiple-listing websites together, printing out details of potential new homes and giggling about heinously decorated apartments you see online ("Black walls? Seriously?"). Turn each appointment into a celebration by enjoying a meal out beforehand so that you're well-fueled and in a proper mindset to home-shop, and looking at each wrong as a step closer to the place that's right.

Another element of celebration: Some of these homes you'll see (with their supertiny kitchens and ugly orange shag carpets) will make you appreciate where you live so much more. So make a point of discussing that together when you're safely home in your small but stylish space. Home-shopping can bring out the gratitude in you both if you let it, and that is where the happiness resides.

When You Finally Find Your New Home

Your realtor has brought you to a winner. Everything is perfect, from the modern kitchen to the spacious backyard, the hardwood floors and the absence of black walls. You just know it when you find it: You are *home*. So share your first kiss in that space as your celebration of finding the jewel of the neighborhood, and celebrate with a little shopping spree (I suggest a "welcome" doormat or some other symbolic item from the home-supply store) as well as a look online at the township's website to check out the prices of membership to the town pool, the locations of gyms and beauty salons, to further imagine the life you'll lead in your new place. The business side of buying or renting a new home is on the way, but, for now, the fun is in celebrating your find—as well as the fact that the long search is over. What will you do with all the extra time you now have in the evenings and on weekends?

Signing for Your New Home Purchase or New Rental

Now it's time to get down to business. If you're buying, that means a bank check, a meeting with attorneys at the closing, getting the "all-clear" from inspectors (which is a celebration all its own), and signing a zillion forms. And if you're renting, that means signing an official lease. It can be exciting but simultaneously terrifying. Newlyweds are *really* going to feel like grown-ups today. You're doing a very big thing together here, so once the ink is dry and the keys are in your hands, it's time for a *big* celebration.

First up is going out to eat. If you're moving to a new area, ask your realtor or neighbors to recommend a restaurant where you'll get lots of local flavor and potentially meet future neighbors. Depending on how far you've stretched to get that deposit money, choose a nice place, dress up, and pop a bottle of champagne to celebrate the fact that you are now home owners. You can do the same with Happy Meals, which some newlywed couples still paying off their weddings say they're equally happy with. It's more about the significance of the event than the cuisine. All that matters is that you *do* celebrate with something, rather than resigning yourselves to a life of ramen noodles and peanut butter and jelly. You may have lean times ahead, but right now, don't miss out on the celebratory meal and a proper toast.

Take a photo of your new house or apartment building, or have someone snap a photo of the two of you in front of the "sold" sign on the front lawn. That's a picture that many newlyweds enlarge and frame— you only get one first house together, so look for these priceless snap-shots. Walk through the house to take "before" pictures of each room if you plan to remodel or redecorate. It's always fun to look back and see your home the way you first glimpsed it, even with all the old-lady furniture and tacky wallpaper. That just makes the "after" photos even better!

Visit the bookstore for books that help you dream about your future in that house. Perhaps a picture-filled volume on container gardening, an instructional book on painting or organizing a home, even cook-books. Again, if you're tapped out on cash, the bargain bins or sale racks often have fabulous books for home buyers, and you get to load up on exciting shared reading material to prepare you for move-in day. This shopping trip at the bookstore is a great celebration, as is a visit to your local library for armloads of *free* resources.

Another shopping celebration: Order your new home address labels now. You get to celebrate designing them, and then celebrate again when they show up in your mailbox. It's official!

Your First Moving Day Together

Moving is exhausting, no matter how big a job you have in front of you. It's physically demanding, emotionally draining, and that mix often makes tempers short, leading to arguments. So consider your celebration to be just getting through each step of the process. Some newlyweds

WHAT ABOUT CARRYING ME ACROSS THE THRESHOLD?

On a busy moving day that included stops at both of your apartments, by the time you get to your house, that carry across the threshold is likely to be rushed and half-hearted. So maybe this is a moment you can take on a day *before* your moving day, such as when you're stopping in to take measurements or let inspectors in. If you're too exhausted to enact the tradition, just hold hands and jump into your house together.

Our New Home

The address of our new home is:

_____

_____

[Attach the printout of the house listing here]

are so stressed, they don't want to be hugged or kissed or interrupted during the process in any way, especially if they're lugging big boxes. So give plenty of personal space to your partner during the actual move, and save the minicelebrations, like hugs, for mutually agreed-upon breaks. Your enthusiasm might annoy him, and his all-business demeanor could dampen your spirits. If you jump out at him with a camera, he may growl at you for being in the way while he's holding a 70-pound box.

So stick with the tasks at hand, and let the little celebrating moments just pop out of your day—like the minute the movers are done and you're catching your breath while surrounded by all those boxes waiting to be unpacked: just a look, a smile, a high-five, a wordless celebration. That's about all you'll have the energy for in the moment. The larger celebration with the champagne or the iced tea toast as the sun sets on your moving day can be when you call it quits, hop into the shower, take your first bath in your new home, or hit the sheets for some shut-eye. Moving day is all about survival.

Why not make your first morning in this new home the real celebration with a lavish breakfast to fuel up for the work ahead?

Your First Vital Records Collection

You may have had to track down your birth certificates and passports for your marriage license and honeymoon travel plans, and now it's time to create your Essential Records file as you combine your lives and organize yourselves. If you choose to change your name after the wedding, you have some heavy-duty paperwork ahead of you, so there's no better time to celebrate your collection of vital documents, including some surprising details you'd be smart to gather now.

First, to make this day of records-hunting more of a celebration than a burden, set up an appointment for a massage or other relaxing treat that evening. You'll work your tail off until then, and then relax into satisfied bliss.

The records you should collect include:

+ Your birth certificates
+ Your social security cards
+ Your bank account information
+ Your credit card information
+ Your credit reports
+ Your medical records
+ Your mortgage or lease papers
+ Your investment paperwork
+ Your IRA or 401(k) information
+ Your car title and registration
+ Your wills
+ Any trust or estate paperwork
+ Living wills or other medical paperwork
+ Your past tax returns

GATHERING YOUR MEDICAL INFORMATION

Right now, each of you should write down on a slip of paper all of the prescriptions you take, including birth control pills, plus any vitamins or supplements, and document any allergies you may have. You'll put a copy of this slip in your wallet and give a copy to your spouse for safekeeping. This way, if either of you has an injury, accident, or illness, that vital info is right at hand for EMTs or for use by emergency room physicians. I know, it's scary to prep for something like this, but it's essential to do this small, important task and have the information on hand.

Set up an organized file in your home office with different colored folders for *His* and *Hers* records. This act stands as a tangible manifestation of the combining of your lives. This is also an expression of trust, knowing your financial history is wide open to your partner, along with your medical history, for optimal communication on both fronts in the future.

When the file is complete, go for that massage, or just take a bath and enjoy the peaceful feeling of having all of your papers in order.

CHAPTER 4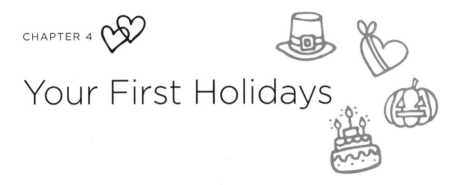

Your First Holidays

This is your first Christmas as husband and wife! All of the traditions you've enjoyed for years take on more meaning, and the holidays can be even more exciting as Mr. and Mrs., especially when you're creating new traditions you'll share for years to come. This is a wonderful chance to begin new traditions that you couldn't add to your individual families "set" observances. *New* is welcome now, so this is the time for creative and meaningful firsts that become the fabric of your shared holidays forever into the future.

The First Religious Holidays at Your Place

You both have so many cherished memories of childhood holidays spent at the homes where you grew up, and now you get to establish your own holiday traditions as a married couple for your first Christmas, Hanukkah, or Kwanzaa. You get to decide where to set up the tree or the menorah, where games will be played, presents unwrapped, songs sung, and you get to decide what's on the holiday menu. The thrill of this celebration is that you get to *combine* your family traditions for food and drink, perhaps bringing in his side's penchant for turkey and trimmings along with her side's traditional filet mignon and seafood. What's important here is that no one feels steamrolled and that no one's traditions are eliminated or overruled by one partner's loyalty to his or her family. We'll address the challenges of a first holiday at home in a later chapter. For now, we're focusing on the excitement of using your china and crystal to set the table, how every day leading up to the holiday can be a thrill of new shopping adventures, such as buying your first set of matching Christmas stockings, or buying a new skirt for the holiday tree, or buying a new menorah together. These are not regular purchases—they're symbolic items that will stay with you as constants on every holiday in the future.

Who's on your guest list? Most newly married couples like to ring in their first at-home holiday by inviting both sides of the family to attend, if possible. Travel during the holidays might be new to one side of the family (or both), so make sure you take extra steps to welcome everyone by setting up a well-appointed guest room and getting welcome gift baskets filled with pampering products for your guests.

When you light the candles and turn on festive music for your guests' arrival, with your home spotless and the meal cooking to perfection, you'll feel like you're in the middle of a dream. You may have imagined this for so long, this fantasy of "our first hosting of an important holiday" that, when it is upon you, it can seem surreal.

Our First Religious Holiday
at Our Place

Our first holiday guests were:

_____

_____

Our menu was:

_____

_____

_____

After our first holiday dinner, we celebrated by:

_____

_____

Celebrate the gathering of family at your table with a special toast to them, explain family rituals so that everyone understands and appreciates the long-held traditions you're honoring by including them in your day, and mark this first holiday in your home by adding a little something of your own, such as the tradition of saying a prayer or playing a specific song, setting a place at the table for departed family and friends or some other symbolic gesture.

It's essential that you bring a touch of your own to this celebration or else you might feel like you're going through the motions, working your butt off to follow other people's traditions. Nothing about this holiday should seem like a burden or a requirement. When you choose the elements you'll use from both of your families, you celebrate keeping it fair between the two of you, and when you add your own traditions in, you start a new thread of future traditions that you can add to in the years to come.

And after the party is over, bring in another new tradition that you'll carry forward. Perhaps you'll warm up some spiked cider and sit together in the darkened living room, looking outside at the snow or just enjoying how festive your home looks. And you'll hold hands in thanks for the blessing you are to each other. Perhaps now is when you'll exchange presents, with the chaos of the holiday dinner over with and your stress level down to zero after your in-laws have left (more on this in a future chapter, too!). Year after year, you can close out your holidays with this moment of quiet, a quenching of thirst, a gift exchange, a small moment of time to absorb the beauty outside or inside your home.

The First Holidays at Your Parents' House

If you spend your first married holidays at the home of your parents, you're bringing a new dimension to the celebration by virtue of your spouse's attendance. Every effort should be made to make him or her comfortable, because this first time missing out on his or her own family holiday is going to be tough. For many people, holidays with the family are sacrosanct, and it's a given in a married couple's life that they'll have to split holidays with their extended families ... unless you're in the rare percentage of couples who take on hosting responsibilities for the holidays, with grateful sets of parents and siblings agreeing to come to you every year. The dividing decision can be a challenge (see pages 213–214 for more on this), or it can be a celebration between the two of you.

Maybe your spouse will be thrilled to spend Christmas at your parents' house in ski country this year. Maybe you'll sit down and agree to spend Hanukkah with your family and Christmas with his. The conversation around how you'll spend the holiday can be as peaceful as you make it, with other factors coming into play: Can you turn the trip to your parents into the first stop on an extended week of travel, visiting with his parents the next few days? Can you make it the first stop on your way to a winter vacation in Hawaii? It may be possible for you to make these family holidays a part of your regular winter getaway, so it's step one of an annual celebration.

When the day arrives, be sure to explain each tradition to your spouse, if he or she has never spent a holiday with your family, and offer him or her their own stocking, ornament, or gifts. It's a wonderful gesture when your spouse gets a say in what goes on that day, since the smallest act of inclusion is a tremendous gift to your marriage. As conversation grows at the holiday dinner table, make sure your spouse is kept in the loop, since no one likes to feel left out of private jokes. You're past the wedding, so catch up with what's going on in the lives of your relatives. Use these events to let your spouse get to know your family even further. You're married now, so in the best of scenarios, your spouse will forge close relationships with your parents, sisters, brothers, their spouses, and everyone else. This is when you celebrate watching those relationships start to grow. That's a deep gift of the holidays that you're celebrating here. How wonderful to see your husband and your brother washing dishes together and talking about football! How amazing to see your mom warm up to your wife, finally, by showing her family photos and collections! It's pure gold. Take some photos!

And, of course, when the merriment is over, the two of you can enact your own holiday traditions, such as sitting by the tree, even if you're not in your own home, so that you honor your own guiding traditions moving forward through your life together.

Your First Valentine's Day

Who says the romance fades once you get married? Not the lucky newlyweds who make it a point to romance each other even *more* now that they've tied the knot. We sigh when we hear about the husband who always brings home two dozen red roses and a box of Godiva chocolates on February 14 even after he's been married for thirty-five years. That's the good stuff of marriage.

So start yourselves on the road to everlasting romance by establishing Valentine's Day rituals on this, your first holiday together with the rings on.

Some ideas to consider:

+ Breakfast in bed, which you've prepared together, with omelettes or French toast, freshly squeezed orange juice, really good coffee, and a rose on the tray. This breakfast doesn't have to be in bed. If you live in a warm climate, it might be out on your terrace for an al fresco start to your day. Some couples reserve this outdoor breakfast *only* for their Valentine's Day tradition.

+ Go for a couple's massage. Check out www.massageenvy.com for local rates on your membership to a massage club that's well-priced and a simple luxury for couples to share on a regular basis. Your Valentine's Day date could include an expert foot massage for less than $20.

- Make a new tradition. Surprise your husband by wearing something new and red. It could be lingerie. It could be a temporary tattoo on your hip. It could be a sexy red lipstick he gets to come home to and mess up.
- Plan a Valentine's Day date. While the restaurants are jammed with young lovers, the two of you can do something unique, such as ice-skating, which you'll then do every year as your tradition. One of the sweetest couples I've ever met made it their Valentine's Day tradition to take a nighttime walk through their neighborhood with travel mugs of hot cocoa, talking about the things they love about each other. They then come home and watch their favorite movie while snuggled up on the couch.
- Start a tradition of writing Valentine's Day love notes to each other, which you can add to your marriage keepsake box.
- Re-create your first Valentine's Day together, even if it was early in your relationship. How fun it will be to return to the same restaurant, and perhaps sit at the same table, now that you're married, reminiscing about that first, nervous Valentine's Day when you had only been dating for a short time and your then-boyfriend didn't know if it was okay to buy you red roses so early in your relationship.

Married Valentine's Days can be even more romantic than your first one. And they should be, since you'll have a life together built on great love. What better time to show it grandly and creatively?

Your First Thanksgiving

The celebration here, if you're hosting Thanksgiving dinner in your own home, is that you can infuse every element of the day with the grander meaning of the holiday: gratitude. So as much as you love that ham and green bean casserole, what you're celebrating is the abundance you're both preparing to share with your families. And from step one down that grocery store aisle, what you're cheering together is your ability to fill your refrigerator, how lucky you are to live in a country where you can walk into a store and grab whatever you need off the shelf, and where food is clean and safe to eat.

So your celebration of this first Thanksgiving centers around a sense of gratitude so deep it can bring tears to your eyes—kind of like the way your emotions overwhelmed you at the wedding. You just have so much to be grateful for in your life.

Here are a few new ways that you can celebrate your first married Thanksgiving:

+ Make it a new tradition, starting now, that you'll give each other Thanksgiving cards. Store-bought cards include some lovely sentiments about gratitude, so agree that you'll each choose a card for the other, date them, and keep them in a special keepsake box for new, annual additions in the future.

+ Some couples choose to make their Thanksgiving cards to each other, either on the computer or even using kindergarten-craft techniques, like tracing your hand on construction paper and gluing on macaroni to resemble a turkey (if turkeys were covered with pasta, that is). That's great for a laugh, and of course that masterpiece has to go on the refrigerator for a while.

+ Together or separately, you can write down the ten things you're most grateful for about your life right now, and after sharing your heartfelt sentiments with each other over dessert or privately after family has left, you can tuck these into a keepsake box. How fun, years from now, to look back and read your own handwriting: "I'm grateful that we finally have a lawn!" or "I'm grateful to have central air-conditioning." Decades later, these are reminders of simpler times when you were first starting out. You only get a first Thanksgiving once, so make it the start of a priceless written tradition.

✼ Take photos of yourselves with the turkey or as chefs in the kitchen. And then make it a ritual to get a chef's photo each year in the future. You can also write down what your menu was and who your guests were each year, scrapbook the wine bottle label, include photos, and add in papers on which your guests have recorded what they're most thankful for.

And, of course, after a great meal comes the great cleanup. You can delay it for a while as everyone fights off the tryptophan turkey sedation, but when it's time to clean, make it a group effort with fun music turned on. No one gets cake or apple pie until the table is cleared of dinner plates and dirty forks and serving platters. Even the kids can help, which is a great lesson to them to see both the men and the women working together as a family.

"Quite often a new marriage means new jobs and a new hometown. If that's the case for you, celebrate this new phase of life with a dish or food local to your new area and share it with those family members coming in from other places. It gets the dinner conversation going about the tastes and history of where you live now. The reverse works equally well. My husband and I were living in Berlin for our first Thanksgiving and we put out a very traditional spread for an international crowd of guests from around the world all of whom were fascinated by the herb stuffing and slow-roasted cranberries with maple syrup."
—Anne Bramley, Cofounder and host of the Eat Feed Podcasts

Your First Birthday Celebrations

This will be your first married birthday cake, your first married birthday card, and your first married birthday gift. What makes this such a special birthday, when you've both always done such a great job of celebrating each other's birthdays through the years before the wedding? You get to buy (or make) the "My Wife" or "My Husband" birthday card this year. You can have those words spelled out in icing on top of the birthday cake, if you wish. It can make the birthday a little bit more special.

Speaking of special, first married birthdays can be planned as five-star extravaganzas with limo rides into the city and dinner at a famous restaurant, a champagne cruise, or a surprise weekend away, or you can go with an "I wish I knew you as a kid" theme, bringing in his childhood love for Spider-Man with kiddie paper plates and streamers from the party-supply store, or show her she's your princess with a Disney Princess theme for décor and cake plates, plus a plastic tiara, plastic glass slippers (hey, that makes you the Prince!), Disney songs playing on the CD player, and an ice-cream cake. Recent newlyweds might go bowling or ice-skating, giving their spouses the dream kiddie parties they never had as kids. You're never too old for this type of celebration, so visit the party-supply store for endless decorating ideas, games, and favor options. You'll never run out of cheesy themes, which makes those getting-up-in-years birthdays sting a whole lot less. Anyone can do roses and a chocolate cake—your first married birthdays together deserve highly creative celebrations that you only get one shot at making special.

The First Time Celebrating Each Other's Religious Holidays

There may not be a T-shirt that says, "I just spent Passover with my wife's family," but a first sharing of a sacred family holiday is something to behold, to mark in time with photos, and extra care given to the dress-up time you'll share at home. Maybe you'll help him with his tie, if it's a formal occasion, and maybe he'll zip up your dress. The getting-ready portion before going to services is part of your celebration! It's showing a great honor to the tradition when you care enough to wear a suit and tie (not everyone does!) or when you get a new dress for the occasion. Families appreciate it when you show up looking your best, too.

The first religious holiday we shared was:

_____

Each moment of a religious ritual is an important occasion, so celebrate sharing them all with your spouse by holding hands or touching him on the arm and smiling to show your appreciation. Again, this may be a wordless celebration, marked with the deep appreciation that your spouse has taken the time to join you. You honor each other's belief systems and values when you show up and are fully present to learn about the service and try everything at the celebratory meal afterward. You're immersing yourself in his or her world, even if you cling tightly to your own religious beliefs and practices. That's a wonderful gift.

Your First Weekend Getaway

Road trip! Sometimes you've just gotta get away, even if your bank accounts are low from the wedding expenses. A weekend or overnight getaway could be just what you need to escape daily stress and enjoy a little romance by the beach, in the mountains, at a bed-and-breakfast, or even at a nearby hotel. No one says you have to fly to get away, and some hotels and B&Bs offer romance weekend packages for less than $100. That makes for a perfect spontaneous getaway with minimal packing and optimal excitement. This will be your first weekend getaway as marrieds, so turn it into a celebration by bringing out your entire romantic reper-toire, from a sexy negligee to chocolate-covered strawberries and cham-pagne, a romantic music soundtrack loaded onto your iPod, and luxuri-ous spa robes and slippers of your own.

This might be the first time you get to use the luggage you received as a wedding gift, so make it a moment when you attach luggage tags with your new married name or address to these suitcases and garment bags. You'll use these for a long time, so make sure you don't let this moment slip by as just an unnoticed task. It's a small thing, but big in meaning. It may take you all over the world, starting with this one simple trip.

Our first weekend getaway was to:

_____

Even if you have just twenty-four hours or less, make your time count. In a resort town, you might go antiques shopping and pick up something for your home, which becomes a part of your romantic history. Get tickets to a museum exhibition, such as a butterfly dome or an art show. Check the city's tourism website for special-event tickets and discounts, research unique restaurants, or find a romantic piano bar where you can request your special song. A get-away doesn't have to be long to be packed with romantic moments.

Your First Big Vacation Since the Honeymoon
What? Another vacation? After that pricey honeymoon?

Sure! Why not? No one said the first vacation you take after the honeymoon has to be as grand as the honeymoon! Have you looked online lately? You can go to Vegas or Bermuda on the cheap, and you might just have a better time during a five-day getaway that's not timed right after one of the most stressful times of your lives.

Newlyweds say that it took about three full days of their honeymoon for them to get the exhaustion out of their systems. So many are like zombies on the honeymoon as they de-stress and attempt to shake off that sick feeling over the money they spent on their weddings. A new trip can be made now with a clear mind, some good financial recovery, and no major exhaustion, and it's not on top of the wedding, so this first vacation together could be a really blissful one.

It could even be a trip to the destination you originally wanted for your wedding, but had to give up due to family pressures to have a big hometown wedding. Newlyweds who pass on their dream destination for the big day love to experience planning a vacation as a married couple, not in preparation of being a married couple. This is their first big vacation planned together while in the rhythm of their new marriage.

You can celebrate this first by sitting down together to research a few of your top destinations, finding where the deals are, and talking

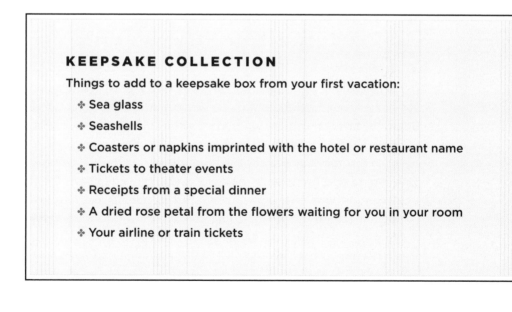

KEEPSAKE COLLECTION

Things to add to a keepsake box from your first vacation:

✤ Sea glass

✤ Seashells

✤ Coasters or napkins imprinted with the hotel or restaurant name

✤ Tickets to theater events

✤ Receipts from a special dinner

✤ A dried rose petal from the flowers waiting for you in your room

✤ Your airline or train tickets

to friends about where they have stayed. Even if it's just one night at the Four Seasons, that could be your first vacation in a five-star resort, which you'll soak up with time spent at the spa, the restaurant, the pool, and the beach. Perhaps your honeymoon package didn't include boating or adventure sports. Now you can celebrate your first upscale vacation months after the honeymoon.

And if the wedding tapped you out, your first vacation could be a romantically spartan one, such as camping in nature. This first, documented by photos and a video, makes for a great story you'll share with your family and friends.

A first vacation planned together opens up the opportunity to start a vacation journal or scrapbook, where you can keep all of your photos and DVDs, plus your own record of the dolphins you saw in the ocean, the bright blue geode you bought at a gift shop that's now on your bookshelf, and the very adventurous cuisines you tried at all of the places you've visited throughout the world. Start now by documenting your first vacation together and you'll always have a complete record that's not missing a thing.

Your First Vacation Sex

We're not talking about honeymoon sex—that's a given. We're talking about the first weekend getaway, the first trip to the beach or to a ski resort, the first not-at-home location for getting naked. For most newlyweds, it's all about location. They've booked a beachfront bungalow at a resort so that they can hear the sounds of the ocean. Or they've booked a penthouse suite overlooking the lights of the city, or a top-notch suite at a ski resort with a view of snow-capped mountains and their own private hot tub on the terrace. Being in a new, luxurious environment is a turn-on, and newlyweds say they plan to keep the spice in their sex lives by taking their act on the road. "How many times can you throw rose petals on the bedroom floor?" is a common statement by those who appreciate the home bedroom seduction scene but would love to make love in front of a fireplace or on a bearskin rug, neither of which they have in their own home.

This gives booking vacations a whole new sexy dimension, doesn't it? And this first vacation you're headed to holds the promise of a big-screen movie-type love scene, planned by you. Using the movie love-scene analogy, you get to create the soundtrack (which is incidentally called "the score" in the movie biz), set the scene with flowers and candles, and choose the wardrobe. Husband can pack his sexiest boxers, and wife can buy a little something naughty and new, or, in keeping with the vacation theme, sexy ski bunny, anyone? Hula girl? Of course, your husband can also get into the act with his own sexy ski instructor getup, or make his entrance into the room wearing only a lei.

Vacation locales might also feed into the menu for your seduction, such as ripe and juicy island fruits to entice your senses. Or try a mango instead. At the beach, you'll find oysters everywhere. You get the idea . . . Play "chef" to your seduction by ordering up an indulgent room service platter.

A VACATION SEX RITUAL

Now's the perfect time to establish an every-vacation sex ritual, such as taking a shower together, which gives you a private, shared history of the best showers you've ever been in: marble in Italy, under a waterfall showerhead in Maui, personalized settings to the water's heat in Aspen, behind glass doors in Spain, and so on. As a married couple, you've just created a long-lasting tradition you can't tell the kids about someday!

You might time your first vacation sex to the sunset or sunrise, whether by the ocean, in the city, or at the mountains, just make sure you're smart about keeping your act private, not out at the pool deck or on a public beach. We don't want you in jail after your first vacation sex! You know better, but some couples need a little reminder. Unless you're on a private island where you can do it anywhere, stick to your suite.

The First Time You Send Out Holiday Cards Together

Have yourself a merry little time with your first holiday cards as husband and wife, which mean that much more if you didn't send joint cards to friends and family in previous years. This moment is a big one for a lot of guys, since they've seen their other married guy friends doing the domestic bliss thing with their new wives, and those "family" holiday cards gave them a little pang of envy during their single days. Surprised? Don't be. Men say they often registered green-eyed moments when their guy friends' lives showed signs of belonging and acceptance, a family of their own, maturity. Hopefully, you married someone who can appreciate a first like this, so that this first holiday card isn't ruined by an ill-timed joke or a request for off-color holiday cards.

It's a festive trip to the mall or the card store, where you'll browse through the selection of holiday cards together. Make sure you choose your couple's holiday card design as a team, since it would be unfair and controlling for one of you to force a style on the other ("This is what we're sending out." "Kittens on a sled? Seriously?"). Take a cue from the post office's supply of holiday postage stamps, perhaps, by choosing one box of religious cards and one nonreligious card set to suit your list of family and friends' own belief systems and their own particular holidays at this time. And why not throw in a box of humorous cards to send to friends who would appreciate the holiday humor? Not everything has to be silver and gold. There are some hysterical cards out there, and if it suits your couple style, go for it. Or maybe you'll make your own card, using a photo from your honeymoon or in your new home.

Now for the sit-down to write them out, sign them, and address them. This is best done with a mug of holiday hot cocoa and whipped cream (use the *good* hot cocoa and surprise him with the big marshmallows) served in oversized mugs that now become your annual "holiday card ritual mugs." You'll use these every year for your tradition of penning your holiday greetings as a team, handing cards back and forth for each other's signatures.

Chances are, you have all of your family and friends' addresses from the wedding invitations and thank-you notes, so the actual addressing should be a breeze.

MAIL CALL!

When the first holiday card addressed to you as a married couple arrives in your mailbox, it's definitely something to celebrate. If you get the mail earlier in the day, wait for your spouse to come home before you tear it open. This is a big moment, your very first holiday card arrival, addressed properly with your married names. Save that envelope and save that card! Better yet, save *all* of the cards you get this year. It's the first and only time you get this first!

The First Time You Buy Holiday Gifts for Each Other

Instead of buying something functional, such as that set of coasters that remains on your registry for 15% off in your completion program, consider turning this holiday gift into something more significant and sentimental—a "keeper" for your future holidays, such as a household item you can pull out every year, the first item in a new collection you've mentioned wanting to start, or some other gift with an evergreen quality to it. This way, the gift is thoughtful, personalized, and carries the celebration of a first in a line of many to come.

While we all love jewelry or a great book, a bottle of perfume or tickets to a concert, those things can be given for any gifting holiday. This is the time for a first occasion present. So make your choices celebration-worthy by selecting items that promise to play a role in many shared holidays in the future, such as pieces for a nativity set, perhaps made of crystal or china. Ornaments are great—inexpensive items to choose if your wallets have been hit by the wedding.

If your faith offers multiple gift-giving occasions, decide now how you'll format the holiday gift-giving plan you'll use in the future. Perhaps you'll give the big gift on the first night and then give really inexpensive gifts on the next nights. This discussion can be especially thrilling, since together you're creating the form of your future holidays, and any future children will grow up with the plan you're setting right now.

Perhaps you'll ring in this occasion with a new holiday journal where you can record the details of your plans, guests, gifts you have given and received, holiday wishes, and plans for future holidays, such as "In 2020, we'll spend Christmas in Paris." A holiday Dream Book is an amazing gift for newlyweds to share. You'll fill those pages year after year with new plans and perfect presents for each other.

The First Time You Buy Holiday Gifts for Each Other's Families

Before you were married, did you give separate gifts to each other's families? Or did you both sign the card given with the gifts you gave to your relatives? If your practice was the former, now is when you decide if you're going to keep that tradition up or if you'll do "couple gifts" to everyone. Is there a big change in your gift-giving method now that you are husband and wife, or is everything going to stay status quo? Some newlyweds say they like to keep their individuality and continue to give personally chosen gifts from them alone, as well as receive gifts *for* them alone from their relatives. So what you're celebrating here is either the change or the no-change. There's comfort in some things remaining unchanged, and maybe you *like* getting gifts chosen for you alone, rather than a household gift to share with your spouse. So what's it going to be? With that decision made, you now have your gift-shopping plan, either going solo or as a team.

The first gift-shopping for your new relatives is a momentous one, and you might be a little bit nervous. Will the in-laws like what you choose? How can you find out if they already have this CD or coffee-table book? What if they want to exchange it? As far as this last question, some people exchange *every* gift they receive. It's just what they do. Nothing personal. Just make sure you include a gift receipt with any gift you give them and they can switch it without ever having to ask you for a receipt (and possibly hurting your feelings, which they would worry about).

Here's a secondary celebration moment: put effort into your wrapping style. Presentation is key, you know, so how you wrap these items says a whole lot to your new relatives: a careful wrapping job with beautifully tied ribbons impresses with a message of, "I cared enough to take the time to wrap this for you." A gift shoved into a gift bag with no tissue paper says, "I threw this in here on my way out to the car just now." Make the good impression so they celebrate their first gift from you as a new member of their family.

Your First Holiday Eve

What are your usual night-before-the-holidays traditions? Each of you might have grown up with holiday eve family dinners, gift-opening sessions, singing, and other festivities that you might carry into your married life now. And those are to be celebrated, especially when you're combining "we have a big meal" with "we exchange one gift the night before" for the perfect blend of your worlds. Again, no one's traditions are eliminated; you're blending so that everyone is happy. The night *before* a big religious holiday could be your main celebration, especially if you're traveling to visit parents or siblings on the holiday. These rituals will become etched into your experience now and in the future.

When the family leaves your place, or when you retire to a relative's guest room, what is your first holiday eve celebration going to be? Here are some possibilities:

+ Take this time to exchange your own gifts with each other, privately, so that you can thank each other with a big, passionate kiss and share the romantic story of why you chose this particular item.

+ Put on your coats and go for a quiet drive through the neighborhood, looking at the houses decorated with holiday lights or at the stars.

+ If it has snowed, bundle up and go out for a peaceful midnight walk together, enjoying the silence and the crunch of the snow underfoot.

+ Sneak down to the kitchen and help yourselves to a turkey sandwich or share a slice of pie.

+ Watch a holiday-themed movie like *It's a Wonderful Life* or *A Christmas Story* on television or on DVD.

+ Put on a great holiday music CD and just sit by the fireplace with glasses of wine.

The idea is to make this the very first in what will become your annual holiday eve ritual. Years from now, you'll always listen to that music CD or watch a holiday classic on TV, or take that drive through the neighborhood, remembering the very first time you did this as husband and wife. It's these holiday traditions that become the glue in your marriage, something rich and beautiful to look forward to no matter how hectic and crazy your holidays get if you have kids or when relatives are scattered across the country. This ritual may become the thing you look forward to the most each year.

Your First Holiday Morning

Remember waking up on Christmas morning at 5 A.M., throwing off the covers, and running downstairs to see all of those presents under the tree? It was sheer bedlam as you and your siblings tore into all of those gifts, wrapping paper everywhere, and the bells and whistles of toys filling the air as your childhood treasures. Remember that bike with the big red bow sitting in the corner?

You may be adults now, but how much fun would it be to *act* like kids on this first holiday morning? Wake up at 5 A.M., throw off the covers, and race each other down the stairs, maybe pulling on his shirt so that you can dart past him in the hallway? Clomp noisily down the stairs to discover the gifts you've set under the tree. Don't they look *so* much better this morning than they did when you set them out? And here's a fun idea: You both might sneak downstairs the night before to set out a special, secret gift by the tree. A wrapped velvet box with jewelry in it? A mountain bike with a big red bow? This first holiday morning together could be your chance to create your spouse's dream holiday morning: You may have told your husband about how you always wanted a Barbie doll with the big pink coat, but your parents never had the money. Well, he can find one on eBay. He may have told you that his parents always gave him clothes for Hanukkah, but he always wanted a pet hamster. Well, that could be the perfect gift now.

The chance to make a childhood holiday dream come true is a priceless first holiday morning celebration for you now. These could be the most remarkable gifts you ever give each other.

Let the wrapping paper fly in pandemonium, or take turns, and then whip up an extravagant breakfast, such as Belgian waffles using your new waffle maker, or eggs Benedict, which you know is the thing he always craves when you go out for brunch. Forget cereal or donuts—this breakfast is going to be something special, including champagne or mimosas (or even your orange juice) in your wedding flutes. If you have a family tradition of making strata, whip one up the night before to enjoy that morning, which is a huge celebration if it's his family's tradition and recipe and this is your first time making it. Take photos of that gorgeous, baked beauty so that you can show his family. It's a gift of love to prepare the in-laws' recipes or to work together on your family recipes for this very special breakfast.

After you eat, it could be your tradition to open the second half of your gifts, or the gifts from your families that were mailed to you, or the stocking stuffers. Splitting this morning into two segments renews the joy for each session and stretches out the excitement of the holilday.

The First Time You Make a Traditional Family Holiday Recipe

If you love to cook and consider your and your spouse's family recipes to be treasures, it's an amazing moment when you prepare these recipes for the first time, together. The holidays are filled with the tastes of home and every memory they evoke, the warm feeling of belonging, and every story each recipe carries with it. It is often a great moment

Our First Holiday Morning

Our first holiday morning wake-up time was:

_____

The first gifts we opened were:

_____

_____

_____

The gifts we received were:

_____

_____

_____

Our breakfast included:

_____

_____

when you tell your spouse that your grandmother always made this salad when you came home from college, or that this bread recipe was the one thing your great-grandmother brought with her when she emigrated to this country . . . it's such a gift to share these stories with each other! The first holiday recipe you make together as husband and wife holds a huge place of honor for you both, and you'll get another celebration when you tell your relatives about your experiences in preparing it—even if something goes wrong, which just makes the story fabulously interesting later on! "I added salt instead of sugar" or "The soufflé did fine as I carried it to the table, and then when I placed it down, it fell!" You may have wanted to cry at the time, but everyone in the family will tell you the same thing happened to them. The fallen soufflé makes you part of the family now! Congratulations!

Back to the kitchen. The act of locating the family recipe may be filled with baited breath, a happily increased heart rate, a bounce in your step. You open your recipe box, and *there it is*. In your grandmother's handwriting, the recipe for almond drop cookies, or that tattered-edge bread recipe that came across the Atlantic on a boat. Recipes are treasures in family lore. Protect that recipe card as you prepare the ingredients: eggs, vanilla, yeast, flour, baking powder. You have all of the makings lined up, and your new silver mixing bowls from your bridal shower ready to go.

This might be the first time you get to use so many of your wedding gifts in the kitchen! You're mixing old family traditions with the abundance of your new life together! Great-grandma may not have had a KitchenAid, but you have her wooden spoon to use now. How awesome is that?

"I just love you so much right now," said one recent newlywed to his bride. "You're all radiant talking about your uncle making this recipe for the family . . . I love that your family means so much to you."

Following a recipe together is an exercise in teamwork, plus a great chance to press up against each other at the kitchen counter. Don't you just love to watch him cook? I think it's one of the sexiest things a guy can do. Proficiency in the kitchen means he can really cook in other areas of his life, right?

Photograph your masterpiece for posterity, and celebrate a job well done with the well-known maxim, Kiss the Cook. A lot.

The First Keepsake for Your Holiday Collection

When you entered this marriage, you may have brought with you a collection of holiday decorations, but this is the first piece you're buying to start off your married collection. Hallmark and other brands offer commemorative "first Christmas together" and "first Hanukkah together" ornaments inscribed with the year, so that's a fine place to start. You can also look into having ornaments inscribed at www.thingsremembered. com so that you can personalize your keepsake to the holiday you celebrate, such as moon and water festivals or saints' days. You'll also find "first home" ornaments if that has been a part of this amazing first year of yours. Each year in the future, one glance at these pretty little ornaments will take you back to this moment in time, to your first holiday together as a married couple. If your religion doesn't have an ornament tradition, you can collect ritual objects, special dishes, or holiday decorations. What's important is that you are collecting items that will be used over and over again to celebrate these special times. These items will be part of your lives every year.

You don't have to stop at this one inscribed ornament, though. It's a wonderful celebration when you pick up the first piece of what will be an ongoing collection. If you dream of a tree with all-matching white ornaments, but it would cost hundreds for you to outfit your collection right now, just get one or two unique and beautiful ones this year. Next year, you may find white ornaments with a silver swirl, or heart-shaped white ornaments.

Our First Holiday Keepsake

Our first holiday keepsake was:

_____

We chose it because:

_____

_____

[Attach a photo]

Why are these minicelebrations so important? It's just hanging an ornament on a tree or setting out a holiday item, after all. What they are is a form of grounding. The holidays can get crazy, especially if you're hosting a family dinner or visiting a lot of relatives. This one quiet moment where you hang or display that new ornament reconnects you to the bright love you share right now. It's a moment's rescue for every nutty holiday season in the future.

CHAPTER 5

Social and Life Events Together

No *marriage is an island*. You have friends and family to share your life with, and that means parties and get-togethers with those you love ... and those you tolerate. They'll be thrilled to see you for the first time as husband and wife, so expect lots of questions along with all of those hugs and congratulations. You'll also have some events that are yours alone, social outings just for the two of you, so don't let these fun firsts slip by you uncelebrated!

The First Family Party You Attend

If the family hasn't seen you since the wedding, their last image of you might have been in your gown and tux—so dress smashingly in something that befits the event *and* your status as stylin' newlyweds. In decades past, women picked out a "going-away" outfit that they changed into right after the reception and it was a *big deal* to choose the perfect suit dress. While that tradition has faded, why not revive it with your own little twist: a *coming-back* dress that you'll wear to the first family party with extended relatives in attendance.

The first family party we attended was:

_____

Of course, you won't celebrate by sharing photos from your own wedding if this is a party in honor of someone else (I can't emphasize this enough! It's rude to steal someone else's thunder), so just promise to e-mail some shots or a link to your online photo album. Then sit back and enjoy this party that someone else has planned *for* someone else, a party you're not responsible for! This is your time to hug and be hugged, subtly let people take a second look at your wedding bands, and catch up with family in the all-important bonding ritual of the family soiree. And if it's a gift-giving occasion, the two of you get to celebrate your very first married couple's gift (or gifts) given to someone else.

The First Wedding You Attend

After all the fuss and excitement and stress of your own wedding—which may still be fresh in your mind—you now get to go to someone *else's* wedding and actually eat some food! Now that's cause for celebration! Even though other guests have a tendency to want to compare this wedding to yours, don't entertain any catty conversations about how much this couple's centerpieces cost ("or *didn't* cost!"). Be gracious by complimenting the couple's choices, especially if this wedding is on a less extravagant (or more extravagant) scale than yours. It's just human nature to compare, but as the kind newlyweds you are, you're appreciating everything you're being treated to as a guest at this wedding.

How does this wedding turn into a celebration for you? It's your first wedding dance out in the real world, with no train bustled behind you. You're in the circle of marrieds among your family or friends now, so you get to hop on that branch of the family tree. You may begin to feel a different vibe toward you now. Many newlyweds say it's their first time treated like an adult at a family gathering. So drink that in and be reminded of the joy you both felt when you took your vows.

After the wedding is when your celebration happens. Any wedding is a chance to remember your own—and celebrate your own union with a glass of wine or champagne, a cake you've bought just for this evening, which you'll cut with your wedding knives (they're not supposed to be one-use only!), and by playing your song on the CD player while you slow dance in the living room. You can tell each other new details of what you noticed or remembered from your wedding day (even if you've heard the first-time-I-saw-you story a hundred times, it's still romantic!), and you can create a new, sexy ritual for *every* time you attend a wedding: change into wedding-white lingerie that night and "play" bride and groom one more time. This time, you probably won't be so exhausted! The wedding night seduction ritual is your secret rendezvous at the end of someone else's big day, and a great way to keep the sizzle in your newlywed mindset.

He'll love it every time another wedding invitation shows up in the mail. You'll celebrate every wedding this way. . . .

The First Family Vacation

If this isn't the first time you're vacationing with one of your families, not much is going to change as far as the actual trip itinerary (except maybe the sleeping arrangements if you used to bunk in separate rooms at your parents' request). If this is the first time you're joining your new family on a getaway, or the first time your spouse is joining your family for its annual beach vacation, you have plenty of opportunities for both shared and private celebrations. The first is, obviously, a celebratory meal when you arrive at your destination, where you'll propose a toast to the family with thanks for including you and your spouse, with hopes for many more shared events in the future. Parents love to hear this! They worry that the annual family vacation will go by the wayside as you take vacations on your own. So if you intend to keep the family vacation tradition alive, now is a wonderful time to clink glasses to a future of wonderful memories in the sun, sand, or snow.

Family meals and toasts aside, the two of you can steal away for some alone time, such as a walk on the beach at sunset where you might pick up the first in your new collection of seashells or sea glass, which you'll keep as your "found during family vacations" treasures. Perhaps you can rent bikes and spend the day taking a tour around, or go for ice cream at a local shop. When you've always vacationed at the same resort town, perhaps at the same rented house each year, you develop your regular haunts and preferences for "the best pizza for miles." Sharing these favorites now is an opening to a very rich part of your background. These places were constants in your life while growing up, and now you're at that same pizza parlor or ice-cream shop with your spouse. Would you ever have dreamed that when you were eight years old? Sounds like it's time to split a hot fudge sundae or sit outside licking pistachio ice-cream cones.

Evenings may be prime time for your couple jaunts, especially if your parents like to turn in early and your siblings prefer to go to the boardwalk or arcade or other local attraction. You can now turn your vacation nights into a new annual ritual. You'll relish having most evenings on your own as a couple, but remember to leave a few nights open for family events. It wouldn't be fair of you to "claim" all the nights, especially if you would be changing the family traditions. Never try to make your hosts adjust their way to yours. Work with the times of day that are open and unplanned.

The First Work Event You Attend

Your work friends are like a second family to you, as your husband's may be to him. They may have attended your wedding and you may socialize with them outside of office hours. When the invitation arrives for an office party, a dinner for a boss, or a company trip to a baseball game, this is a very big deal, worthy of a big celebration.

You're attending as wife or husband, or bringing the new wife or husband as an introduction to your "work crowd." And how each of you reflects on the other may be incredibly important to your careers. It's said that some bosses take "family men" and "family women" more seriously on the job, and they assess the spouses of their workers carefully. So take this opportunity to really impress your spouse's colleagues and bosses, or have your coworkers and bosses impressed by your spouse, by getting ready for this event, brushing up on colleagues' names ("Your boss's wife's name is Colleen, right?"), and finding out which coworkers just got engaged and who is expecting a baby so that you can congratulate them.

If this is a gift-giving party, such as the boss's birthday, stop by the liquor store to pick up a fine bottle of wine, and get a second one for your own collection or later enjoyment. Throw in some gourmet chocolates or snacks, and wrap the gift beautifully for a nice presentation. Everything you do, everything you say, registers with everyone at the office, and you may be an object of scrutiny if this is your first time ever attending an office event together. So don't sit in the corner and pick at your food. And don't cling to your spouse like you're terrified of everyone at the party. Mingle. Introduce yourself naturally, not like you're at a networking event trying to make contacts to sell stuff to.

You'll make a great impression. Your spouse chose you for a partner for good reason. After the party, celebrate by showing him what you wore *under* the dress you chose to impress his bosses. You chose *this lingerie* to impress *him*. He'll be amazed that you had that sexy lingerie on all night, and it was your seductive little secret until now.

Your First Time Out with Friends

The first time you go out with your friends after the wedding, you're going to notice a bit of a difference. Now, we have a bunch of factors in play here. Are you attending on your own or with your spouse? Is this a girls' night out or a couples' dinner with all married people? Are you the first to marry, somewhere in the crowd of marrieds, or the last to marry? It will matter in the group dynamic, because any major life transition among friends injects a difference between you. If you were all single girls out on the town before the wedding, your wedding might have registered a shockwave through your circle of friends. You have something they don't have. You're no longer a part of their dating scene. You might not want to go out drinking until 4 A.M. anymore. You're settled and secure, so they may feel insecure by comparison. So let's start off with the scenario that you're out with the girls without your spouse, and you're among the first to be married.

My first time out with friends was:

_____

_____

You can turn this into a celebration by being the person they know and love—not some completely different persona with a ring, a husband, and a house who has no sense of humor anymore. Don't talk all about your wedding or how great marriage is unless they ask about it. They're over your big day. They want *you* back, especially if you were a bit of a Bridezilla, and they've been patiently waiting . . . This is where the celebration happens—you're *back*! Laugh off the wedding stress you were under and allow them to poke fun at anything you were too dramatic about (friends are allowed to quote you, mock you, and pick at you out of love). Make it up to them by buying a round or buying dessert, and then raise your glasses to the end of your reign of terror as The Bride (even if it wasn't such a frightening reign of terror). And then launch into asking them what's going on in their worlds. They'll be so pleased that the person they know is once again among them.

I realize I've painted a very rosy picture of the "return to your social life with friends" first, and that the difference you and your friends feel may be more palpable. For some, the difference is just too great, and tension turns to distance. Maybe being single was the only thing you had in common with some friends. Maybe a friend can't get over her envy of your marriage. As unfair as that is, it still hurts to be on the outside of a group you belonged to for years.

Hopefully, that's not your situation and you find yourself not only celebrating your return to your circle of friends, but also solidifying your bond with them further by establishing a more regular girls' or guys' night out in the future. Maybe once a month works best for everyone, since it's so good for you to have a circle of supportive, fun friends and a life of your own apart from your spouse. Friendships are a very valuable part of life, and it's an investment in your happiness and health to keep yours going strong. So that makes this first time out with them all the more important.

Your First Private Time with the In-Laws

You've always visited with your in-laws together with your spouse before you were married, and now that you're in the family, you may find yourself invited to an event sans spouse. If you've never done this before, it can be a little bit nerve-wracking. Stop worrying about saying something wrong and plan to celebrate this first big honor of family inclusion. You can perhaps:

- Bring a wonderful gift, such as flowers, a vase, a set of coasters, or something for the home as a present for the host. This classy move is always a great way to start.

- Offer to cook something for the meal, or pick up a delectable dessert as your way of contributing. Ask first, of course, because you do want to learn "their way" of doing things. Sometimes families have a set routine of who brings their famous apple pie and who brings their in-demand lasagna. You don't want to walk in there with an apple pie of your own or you might be perceived as competing (even if you're not!).

- Bring a bottle of wine or a special liquor for the event.

- Let them know how happy you are to be included with a simple hug and a thank you in some private moment, such as while you're in the kitchen prepping an appetizer, and

> **GUYS' TIP**
>
> One of the best gifts you can give your wife is making an effort to connect with her family—and she's advised to do the same with your family! So ask her for some suggestions on topics you can discuss with her father, or which type of flowers her mom likes so that you can bring her a bouquet, or maybe you'd like to cook something for the family dinner. The extended family plays a big role in your future, so mark this first married visit with them by taking an action to *show* the in-laws you like them and want to bond.

not in some scene-stealing toast that can wreck an event thrown in someone else's honor.

+ Have a collection of stories ready to go. You want to be able to participate in any conversations, not sit there quietly with your "new to the group" status on display. If you can contribute an anecdote, you're fitting in well. Ask your spouse for topics that will be welcome in the group setting.

+ Find out in advance about any hot topics you need to avoid, as well, such as politics or religion. Any family has its differing views, and you don't want to step on a land mine by talking about politics when that has been carefully avoided in this group.

+ Obviously, don't get drunk and don't totally pig out on the food. Table manners are a big issue with some parents, and they will notice if you lick your fingers at the table. Be prepared to be in the spotlight every second of this event, so bring your A Game.

+ Plan to celebrate this big first with your spouse afterward, perhaps by telling him or her all about how much you enjoyed the event, what you loved on the menu, how much you loved the host's home. He or she *will* hear their family's version of your visit, so it's wonderful to supply your positive feedback for the inevitable relaying later.

The First Sporting Event You Attend Together

If you attend sporting events, whether it's professional football games, minor-league baseball games, or college basketball games, together, this fun day at the stadium or field shouldn't pass by without a celebration of it being your first time there as husband and wife! "Honey, it's our first time being patted down by security together as husband and wife!" may not sound like a line from a romantic greeting card, but isn't it a thrill to turn this regular, been-here-done-that event into a full-on smile-fest when every part of it is something new? Your first hot dogs as husband and wife. His first time waiting outside the ladies room for his *wife*. Your first Mr. and Mrs. foam fingers to wave in the air. The first time you chant "*De-Fense!*" together as husband and wife. He's always loved it when you got into a game, or maybe you've always loved it when he gets into a sport you grew up with.

Do you have season tickets where you're always in the same seats? Or can you get somewhat pricier seats down by the court for this first game together? One newlywed guy reported that his wife got him courtside tickets as a wedding gift— *and* his bound-for-the-Hall-of-Fame hero high-fived him after the game. "That made my *lifetime!*" he said. "I got Shaq sweat on me!" For him, this first was so much better than watching from way up in the nosebleed seats. His wife made it happen. What can *you* make happen for your first sporting event attended together? Can you get VIP seats? How about VIP parking to avoid that long walk or shuttle ride through the parking lot with the masses? Can you get him a team jersey with his favorite player's name on the back?

The first sporting event we attended was:

_____

_____

Even a $5 keepsake baseball from the gift shop can become a treasure. "That was from the first game Mommy and Daddy attended together as husband and wife" could be something you say to your little sports fans someday.

The First Sporting Event You Play Together

This is a fun one, even if you're not the competitive types. You might think of minigolf and bowling as great ideas for a first or second date, but married couples say these are great, inexpensive dates to go on to shake up the routine of daily life. You might even make a bet with one another—winner gets a back rub. Again, the couple who plays together stays together. Will it be minigolf or real golf? Tennis? Bowling? A game of H.O.R.S.E. at the basketball net in your driveway? "Honey, let's play a game" may be the opening bell for your first Mr. vs. Mrs. competition. You can get *really* into it by making it a big event, complete with a little trophy that you buy at the party-supply store, or by purchasing a medal for the winner. Going over the top with these little details is what makes a Sunday afternoon tennis match extraspecial as you celebrate a first in a big way. You can turn this competition into an annual event! One newlywed couple started a tradition of playing minigolf every Fourth of July, and now it's become a family tournament that includes their kids. And their kids invite their friends to play along, too. So this first game of yours could eventually turn into the 25th Annual Family Minigolf Tournament one day . . .

But this year, being the first, all you need is a healthy dose of good sportsmanship, mixed with a little good-natured teasing of your opponent as you psych him out. *You're fun to play with*, he'll probably be thinking, which only adds more glue to your partnership. If he wants to golf again some other weekend, he'll be more likely to ask you to join him, after all. So there is some forward-thinking involved here. You're making play a part of your future.

And if you're *good* at minigolf or bowling, he'll be impressed. If you're bad, he'll appreciate that you tried and got so excited about knocking down three pins. High-fives all around!

The First Time You Play a Video Game Together

You might be at home with the PlayStation plugged in or you might have ducked into an arcade when the rain started during your beach vacation. We're a nation of gamers now, so plan this first celebration as a way to share each other's passion for Madden Football or go old-school with Donkey Kong or Frogger. You'll be amazed at the array of games out there, and in the arcade you can drive against each other, shoot zombies together, and out-ninja each other. This is one of the most surprising firsts that newlyweds enjoy, but it's not surprising that you're mixing a loved pastime, the natural humor that happens when you're just learning how to work the controls, and relaxation time together. That's a recipe for the start of a shared hobby that pays benefits beyond what you would expect. How does boosting brain power sound? Or increased hand-eye coordination? Would you ever have known that you're a great shot with taking out those zombies?

The first video game we played together was:

_____

Great marriages are strengthened by the ability to step out of the world of adult responsibility to just play for a while. It's why we go on vacations. Playing video games might not be your initial idea of romance for when your spouse walks in the door at the end of the workday, but here's an

Stock up on new games every once in a while, and check for rental delivery services or free games at the library. You don't have to sink $20 into every new game on the market. And as an added bonus, you now both have ideas for those just-for-no-reason gifts you like to bring home to each other.

important lesson for newlyweds: Everyone needs downtime when they get home from work. Without it, you get snippy comments, arguments, or silence and isolation; frustration that your partner doesn't want to just jump right into organizing the basement with you. These are all evidence that you haven't established a great decompression ritual.

And that decompression ritual could be your shared hobby of playing video games for a little while. You're never too old to play: as the saying goes, you get old from not playing enough.

Set up your living room or den for a first tournament, perhaps with chips in bowls, sodas or beers chilled and in a bucket, and pizza at the ready. One of my favorite ideas is to find retro T-shirts with video game graphics on them, like Ms. Pac-Man. Slip into your shirt with a cute pair of boy-shorts and you are every gamer's fantasy woman. Guys say they love being accepted by their women, even for so-called dorky traits they have, so if you welcome him home as Sexy Mrs. Dorky, you've just celebrated a very entertaining first for your new marriage and your future.

The First Concert or Play You Attend Together

Did you score tickets to the big concert of the year? That alone is cause for celebration, especially if you logged onto Ticketmaster for that 1.2 seconds before all the tickets were gone. Your fast fingers got you two prime tickets to the most in-demand show. That's worth a hug, a squeeze, a high-five, and the price of whatever fan club you had to join to get access to the tickets on that day. Whatever the cost, you've got a golden ticket, and it's not to a chocolate factory. (But just try to stop singing that song right now!)

You may have attended lots of concerts and plays over the years, but this is the first one you go to as husband and wife. Too many newlyweds let the momentousness of this occasion pass them by. They just grab their tickets and head out to the concert hall, take in the show, and call it a night. But you have far better plans. Be the overdressed couple

MONEY, HONEY

Here's a little tip for money-crunched newlyweds: You can go to the five-star places, but just have a drink and an appetizer at the bar.

there. With him in his best suit and you in a sexy little red dress and high heels, you're showing that you're making this an *occasion*.

Don't just go for dinner before the show—go someplace *new*. Try an exotic restaurant that you've never been to before, maybe a Thai or Moroccan restaurant. Go for drinks at that wonderful little French place you can't afford to eat at.

At smaller concert venues, some artists open themselves up to the audience by signing copies of their CDs. Wouldn't it be wonderful to have your favorite performer sign a CD to you *using your married names*: "Best Wishes to Mr. and Mrs. Joe Smith," for instance.

Even if you can't get backstage to have Sting sign your T-shirt (or a body part), pick up those goodies at the venue as keepsakes for the first concert or play you attended together, and make it a regular date night in the future to take in the big and small shows in town. Keep in mind the fact that many newlyweds often make concert or theater tickets their #1 choice for birthday and holiday gifts.

The First Day You Both Have Off from Work

Who doesn't love getting a day off from work and spending it however they please? Whether it's a national holiday or a personal day you decide to take, these twenty-four hours are yours to plan as you wish. As newlyweds, you might decide to "play hooky" together, especially if it's going to be a wonderful weather day, and give yourselves a three-day weekend with a getaway or an "us weekend" spent at home.

No rushing to do errands. No to-do lists. No work e-mails. How will you celebrate your first married day of free time? How about some of the following:

+ No alarm clock. Wake up at 10 a.m. for the first time since you were in college.

+ Go for a couple's massage at a spa.

+ Drive to a scenic spot and ride bikes or walk by the river together.

+ Go to a local park and just lay out in the sun (sunscreen is important, though, so slather up!).

+ Catch a matinee movie, which is often half-price.

+ Paint a room together. Yes, we said no to-do lists, but if the crush of half-done home projects is stressing you out, this free day to complete home décor jobs is going to become quite the celebration at the end of the day.

+ Take an afternoon nap together. Nice cool, clean sheets, the shades drawn to block out the light, you both in your spooning positions, and this afternoon siesta can be a real snooze celebration for the sleep deprived.

+ Order in some great food and watch great movies all day. Do you have a boxed set of DVDs from your favorite TV series, or a movie trilogy that you can take in today? Make some popcorn, settle in on the couch, pull a comfy throw over you, and get lost in some great movies.

The First Snowfall

If you live in a place where it snows, you might be one of those people who welcomes that first snowfall with the excitement of a child. Never mind the slush, the ice, having to shovel, having to drive to work in this mess . . . The first snowfall can be magical, so you push the window curtains aside and just marvel at the show going on outside.

This is your first snowfall during your marriage, so document it with plenty of photographs. One newlywed guy trekked down the driveway and halfway up the street to take digital shots of the house covered in snow because he knew his wife was collecting photos of their first garden, the first autumn leaves in front of their house, the befores and afters of the rooms they're redoing. "I just snuck out there and took the shot, to surprise her when she got out of the shower. She was almost in tears when she saw it," he says. His wife reports that his thoughtfulness and sweetness in knowing she'd love that first snowfall photo at their new home was something she told *all* of her friends about, and rewarded him for greatly.

Even if you don't have a house to take photos of, this first snowfall can bring out the little kid in you. So call out, "Snow day!" especially if the weather does preclude you from going to work, and rush to get into your jacket, gloves, and boots. Then run outside together (forget what the neighbors will say) to play in the snow! Snowball fights, making snow angels, building a snow fort, riding down the slope of your front lawn in a toboggan . . . these are the great, fun moments of the young and the young at heart. A fresh-fallen snow gives you a playground of your own, which you can enjoy with youthful and silly activities, or turn it into the celebration of your first walk in the snow, holding hands. Or you can wait until the evening hours, bundle up, and head out for a walk in the pristine snow-covered streets, waving to neighbors who are shoveling their driveways or walks, enjoying the silence. As a newlywed couple with a busy, hectic life-style, this dose of silence and beauty can be a balm to your overstimulated minds. Your celebration of this beautiful moment is also a balm to your souls—and definitely something to note as a first in your marriage.

Relationship experts say that men are more likely to open up in deep conversations during walks or long car rides when they're not looking you in the face or seated in a "serious conversation" position at home. So this might be an added perk!

End your evening with some hot cocoa by the fireplace, or with a hot shower together, or a toe-warming bath with holiday-scented candles and a hot toddy. Do you have one of those packages of pre-made cookie dough? Why not warm up the house with your first batch of holiday cookies right now, marking this first snowfall as the date of your very first baking night? It takes twelve minutes to produce a batch, so it's ridiculously easy to whip up a plate of warm chocolate chip cookies you can enjoy together. This may be the start of your holiday season, too, so you've just made this snowfall day your kickoff to a season of festivities, baking, gifting, and peace on earth. It'll get crazy soon enough with the family visits and holiday meals and wrapping and holiday travel, so this is your moment of quiet and warmth. The first you'll reminisce about in a long future together.

CHAPTER 6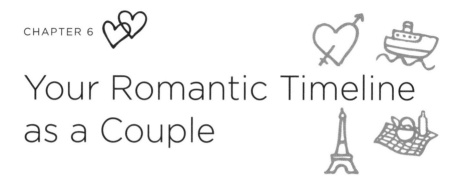

Your Romantic Timeline as a Couple

You're not just limited to the anniversary of your wedding. As newlyweds, your life can be so much more romantic when you celebrate all of your special firsts along the entire history of your relationship. That keeps the romance going and gives you lots of extra reasons to acknowledge how happy you are together, and how much you appreciate each other. These are opportunities to look back on how far you've come, and dream of your future together.

The First Anniversary of When He Popped the Question

You know the date by heart. He planned a beautiful proposal for you, and it was a dream come true. While no other romantic evening will ever compare, the anniversary of when he asked you to marry him now becomes as great a celebration in your partnership as any birthday or holiday. Too many newlyweds think their wedding anniversary is the only big day that counts in their history together, but as you'll see in this chapter, there are *lots* of momentous occasions in your love story that grant you the opportunity to plan a romantic dinner or getaway weekend, get a gift or card, pick up flowers, or any other large or small gesture that says, "This day is important to me." Don't let the anniversary of your engagement fade away in your mind. When you mark it for a celebration, you get an extra anniversary to have some fun, an extra chance to dress up and go out on the town, a special day on the calendar that is for the two of you alone.

The first anniversary of our engagement was:

_____

Here are some ways to make the anniversary of your engagement day a bright spot in your year, a day rescued from the same old thing into something special:

❖ Go back to that same restaurant where he proposed and have dinner. If possible, sit at the same table you sat at then.

❖ Go back to the same spot on the beach or scenic area where he proposed and have a picnic—perhaps the same type of picnic he planned for your proposal.

❖ Flowers are always a great touch. Get the same kind of flower that played a part in the proposal, and add an extra one to the bunch to signify this year you've spent together. Each year, you'll add another bloom to the bunch.

✤ Have a champagne toast using the same glasses he arranged at the proposal. It's always a wonderful symbol to use the same items from that day. Can you spread out the same blanket he set down on that beach at sunset? If you can't get to the beach, just set it on your living room floor and have a picnic at home, or take it outside to the lawn.

✤ If your anniversary falls on a weekday, start that day off with breakfast in bed.

✤ The first one home from work that day lights candles and preps the house for a seduction. Turn on some great music, change into something alluring, set out some chocolate-covered strawberries or other indulgent treat, and listen for the sound of his or her key in the front door lock.

✤ Look back through your photo albums to revisit the pictures from your engagement. Even now, a year or more later, there might be a story you didn't share, such as how paranoid you were about losing the ring box on your way to the restaurant. If you have the big moment on video, sit back and watch that great

GUYS' TIP

Here's a romantic idea that will make this day even more special: write a *new* script for proposing to your wife and ask her to marry you all over again. Maybe you had some ideas in your first draft of the original proposal that didn't make it into the big moment back then, but you can say them now. Or, perhaps the way she handled all of that wedding-planning stress really impressed you, and you'd like to tell her now—in this great, romantic place—just how much you admire her. Your words will mean so much to her.

footage again today, and if you journaled your thoughts on the experience, read to your spouse the exact words you wrote while still in the rosy bliss of the new engagement.

The Anniversary of Your First Date

By now, you might not know this exact date, so look back through the e-mails you may have kept between the two of you to 1. *Find out* the date, and 2. *Print out* those e-mails as the most sentimental and romantic gift ever. Did you keep all of the e-mails from your earliest dating days? Now *that* would be a treasure! If you don't have the e-mails, do you have an old calendar where you wrote "Date with Jim" on a particular Saturday night? It's incredibly fun to flip through old calendars to see the exclamation points you wrote next to "Skiing with Jim!" when your first getaway was planned, or the six days in a row that you had plans with Jim.

Once you have your anniversary date, revisit that first date. Was it a dinner or drinks date? Go to that same restaurant or bar where you had that first date, ordering the same things or splitting an appetizer the way you didn't have the courage to do during your first date. You were too enthralled with the conversation and didn't get around to ordering food! Or, you really wanted that molten chocolate cake but didn't want to order it on a first date (what would she think of you?!). Here's your chance to have that first date again: hold hands across the table, order whatever you like, not minding if your feet touch under the table (or make *sure* that your feet touch under the table). First dates can be nerve-wracking, so here is your chance to celebrate not only getting through it successfully, but also being right back here as a couple in love—with none of those first-date jitters.

Or, have some fun with a new plan for a first date do-over: "Here is the place I *wish* I could have afforded to take you to on our first date" opens the door to a five-star restaurant overlooking the ocean, with waiters who place the napkins on your laps, fine gourmet food on the menu, a sommelier who comes to your table to explain their wine choices. Back in your single-and-dating days, your first date sites weren't necessarily so posh, and as much as you loved having margaritas and nachos at a chain restaurant that night, *this* is the place you wished you went.

On the flip side of redoing your first date, you can turn it into a laugh-fest by planning the cheesiest first date ever, going all-out to plan a date that would never have gotten you a second look back in your earliest dating days. What's the cheesiest first date plan you can imagine? Roller-skating? Going to see a trashy movie? The idea is to plan a date that gets you both laughing in an "I would *still* have wanted to go out with you again if you planned this date back then" kind of way. It would have been a leap of faith, though, wouldn't it?

Our first date anniversary plans included:

_____

_____

How fun to plan an intentionally cheesy date!

Your Six-Month Wedding Anniversary

In effect, you're celebrating your *half*-anniversary, so the theme for this celebration is *half*. That means getting half a cake (you can find these cake halves already created and packaged at your supermarket, or make your own), half a carafe of wine at a restaurant or at home, serving half a lobster (make it the good half: the tail), or a half rack of ribs. Creative chefs can do the following:

❖ Cut a head of lettuce in half, then halve it again and serve it with cut veggies and dressing as a theme side dish.

Our Six-Month Anniversary

Our six-month wedding anniversary
was:

_____

We celebrated it with:

_____

_____

_____

* Serve the meal on one half of the plate and dot delicious sauces on the other side of the dish for theme and presentation points.
* Do a combination platter with half beef and half seafood: surf'n turf fits the theme of *half*.
* Cut fruit slices in half for a themed dessert.
* Fill dessert cups halfway with chocolate mousse, or create full parfait cups with half chocolate and half vanilla pudding or mousse.
* For drinks, small coffee cups for espresso or cappuccino work

perfectly with this theme, since they often measure about half a cup of coffee—so why not end your meal with half a mini espresso cheesecake and fire up your new cappuccino maker for this important celebration.

And all food aside, you can certainly carry the *half* theme into the rest of your evening, by wearing half of a sexy lingerie ensemble. *Which* half is up to you. And at this point, I suggest forgetting about the half theme, since no one wants half a seduction!

Your First Time Back to the Most Romantic Place of Your Past

Make it a point to go back to the most romantic place of your shared history. It might be the restaurant where he proposed, the bed-and-breakfast you went to as your first couple's weekend getaway ever, the resort where you took your first big vacation together, the site of your first kiss—even if your first kiss was in the parking lot after your first date! Go back there, stand in that same spot, and plant one on each other the way you wish you could have the first time!

When you revisit the romantic places of your past, you revive those wonderful memories within you and between you. How amazing to be back in that same spot now as newlyweds! And how amazing to think of all the things that have happened and all the places you've been together since then! Consider this a homecoming to the scene of your first kiss, the place where you first realized you were in love, the setting where it struck you—this is *The One*. And soak that in.

Share with your spouse all of the thoughts you had back in that moment, the first time you were there, and how he or she has made the future even better than you ever dreamed it could be. And just like that moment, *this* moment will be filled with your wishes and dreams for your future together. Imagine how you'll feel the next time you come back!

The Anniversary of When You Moved in Together

For too many newlyweds, this date passes by uncelebrated. It's just another day on the calendar; another day to walk the dog, vacuum the living room, do the food shopping. *Yawn*. But when you claim this anniversary day for a celebration, you infuse it with an element of excitement, romance, and seduction—and an appreciation for the home you've built together. That can be the key to your celebration this time, focusing on a *then* and *now* gratitude that there are no mountains of boxes in the kitchen. The bedroom is painted and organized. All of your stuff has a place (hopefully). And you're filling this home with wonderful memories, such as those that took place during your wedding weekend.

Call it a "We're Home!" party, and the only boxes you carry or open will be the gifts you give each other. Make them gifts for your home, the items you've both looked at in catalogs or online and said, "Someday we'll get that cherry wood letter organizer for the kitchen" or "In the spring, we'll get a funky new welcome mat for the front door." The anniversary of really being home is the perfect time to surprise each other with the fun or functional items to decorate your place. If your bridal registry is still active, as most are a year or two after the wedding, log back in there and pick out something you both wanted at the time of your wedding. It doesn't have to be anything expensive or elaborate, just an "I know you wanted this" gift given in celebration of this big day in your romantic timeline.

The theme of "putting down roots" opens up the possibility of marking this day by planting a tree out in the front yard or planting flower bulbs, giving your spouse a container gardening book to prepare for the spring planting season, or just buying a little green houseplant. A living gift in the form of a tree or plants or flowers is one that grows along with you, a very symbolic way to celebrate this day.

And don't forget the fact that you are not working your butts off like you were back on moving day. Celebrate *that* with a day of relaxation, a back rub, a bubble bath—the leisurely life.

The First Time You Watch Your Wedding DVD

Make sure that your first time watching your wedding DVD is an event shared by the two of you alone. Without a roomful of parents, siblings, and friends at a video-viewing party (there's plenty of time for that later!), you can take in far more details, hear your own vows, and watch it in peace without everyone else's comments and observations. A lot of your ceremony is going to be quite new to you, since you may have been too nervous to even hear the words of the readings—or even your vows! This first viewing of your wedding video is your own private celebration between you and your spouse.

Pop open some champagne if you wish to bring in the bridal theme, and enjoy a special moment where you clink glasses *now* at the same time you're clinking glasses in your wedding video. Or pour some wine, if you don't feel like champagne. Or have root-beer floats for this viewing party, if that's what you're craving, and make it a "we're comfy in our pajamas" evening.

You can create a theme meal of hors d'oeuvres similar to the ones at your wedding, only it's okay if these were bought in the frozen food section at the supermarket. Add some shrimp cocktail and you have a little wedding-style buffet of your own set up for picking during the show. Some couples choose to go comfy with an ordered-in pizza, just to eliminate any fuss with cooking a meal. Tonight, it's all about the wedding DVD.

As the video starts, make sure *you're* not the annoying person in the room with too many comments, keeping the other from hearing what's going on in the footage. A big mistake is being too vocal, missing the first dance footage because you're yapping about the video editor not including the receiving-line footage. You can watch this DVD a thousand times. For now, make your celebration an almost-silent one as you drink in every detail, squeezing your partner's hand when you see something wonderful (like your first kiss)—and, of course, you can kiss at the same time as your images on the video.

One way you might want to celebrate your first video viewing is by standing up and slow-dancing to *your song* right there in your living room as you watch yourselves on the screen. Make it a pact that every time you hear your song, you'll stop what you're doing and dance together just a little bit. That's the gift and the great celebration of watching your video for the first time alone. You get to make promises for future traditions related to your wedding.

This wedding DVD becomes even more valuable over time, especially during any rough patches that might lie ahead. When life presents you with tough times, or if conflicts arise between you, being able to revisit your wedding day with this DVD might bring your perspectives back to where they should be. In the middle of work or money stress— whatever challenges you face—you can look back on this day, see your smiling faces, see the tears in your eyes, listen to the words of your vows, and really remember who your spouse is. Wedding DVDs are a tool against complacency, a tool against taking each other for granted, and a gift for every day in the future.

If you have postwedding blues right now, as some newlyweds do, the DVD may hold another lesson for you: What was most beautiful that day was the way you both looked at each other—not the flowers or the cake or everyone dancing . . . it was about your love for each other. You can see it right there on the screen. So you can snap yourself out of your postwedding blues and look into your spouse's eyes. You have, and will always have, the most important part of that day right there with you.

Your First Romantic Date Out on the Town

The romance doesn't have to fade after the wedding! That's a fallacy created by people who let their own romances fade. You have to put in a little bit of effort and exercise some creativity. It all starts with planning dates for each other.

Newlyweds can establish another terrific tradition for their "happily ever after" by taking turns planning romantic dates for each other. Here's how it would work: One of you calls the other on the phone (no texting allowed!) to ask the other out on a date. "I was wondering if you would like to go to dinner with me this Friday night" is perfect—very chivalrous if you're the guy, very flattering if you're the woman. You'll be returned to your early, electrically charged courting days by treating your partner like a person you're trying to impress.

With the date set, make it a fun celebration when you're the asker by sneaking outside as your spouse is getting ready and ringing the front doorbell. He or she opens the door and there you are with a bouquet of flowers. That's dating gold! This one simple gesture will mean the world to your partner, since it's probably stepping out of your daily routine. Set this First Date night apart from any other event. It should be a dress-up event, not a jeans and sweater night.

Chivalry is in order during this date, no matter who has done the asking. Guys, open the car door for your wife. During dinner, ask what she would like and order for her when the waiter arrives (and ladies, please don't take this as any affront to your own ability to order—it's just a traditional sweet thing that old-fashioned guys like to do.) Propose a toast to your date, and promise many more in the future.

And when the meal is done, you might want to surprise your spouse with a stop at another location, perhaps a piano bar that offers slow-dancing, or take a walk by the waterfront after getting cappuccinos "to go" from a nearby coffee shop. When you go to the after-dinner location, you're showing that you've given this date a lot of thought; you've really considered what would make his or her night.

And as you walk by the waterfront, or even back to your car, holding hands, look around at all of the couples that you would guess are on their first date or an early-in-the-relationship date. Remember when *you* were just starting out? Remember the first time you walked holding

WATCH OUT!

Newlyweds often complain that their partners dress down too often now that they're married. It's a comfort thing, but it can come off like a laziness thing. Take your mother's advice and "always look your best." Relationship experts—and every magazine article on keeping a relationship strong—say that taking care of yourself and making an extra effort to look and feel your best is a great investment in your marriage. So get out your sexiest, best dress and knock his socks off. Men, put on your sharpest suit and watch her swoon.

hands? Pull each other a little bit closer as you make your way home, and then invite your spouse inside for a nightcap. You both know what that means.

The First Night You Sit Down to Write Wedding Thank-You Notes

After all of those wonderful, generous wedding gifts have come in, and after you've experienced your guests' generosity of their time and travel efforts to be at your wedding, a great thank you is a must, but most brides and grooms, after the exhaustion of the wedding preparations and the new adjustments to married life, dread the overwhelming task of having *so many* thank-you notes to write. Some procrastinate, leaving their guests wondering about their level of class, and some dive right in with a plan to blast through all of them in one evening. Both plans can be big mistakes.

A wiser plan is to break the task into several different evenings of sitting down to write twenty or thirty notes at a time, so that you're fresh while writing them and not just delivering blasé "Thank you for the generous gift" messages to the last 150 of your guests. This job should be a great gift, not a burden! So make it three or four nights of celebration, based in a mindset of genuine gratitude. Each name on your list is a valuable loved one who cared enough to support you in your future life together. Here are some ways to turn this first night of thank-you writing into a celebration of just how rich the two of you are:

- First, be flexible about timing. If you set Thursday night as your first thank-you note writing session, but one of you comes home from work tired, cranky, or sick, cancel the "party" and choose another night. Neither of you should be forced to undertake such an important, meaningful yet labor-intensive task when you're not up for it. Pick another night with no complaints or pressure.

- Next, be well-fueled. How about making a fabulous home-cooked meal—your favorite comfort food, and a sweet dessert saved as your reward for after you get the first twenty cards written? Newlyweds might get a few 2-pound lobsters steamed at the grocery store, and serve them with a refreshing salad, as a celebratory meal. Don't load up on the wine, since drunken note-writing is a recipe for disaster. Yes, wine can be your drink for the evening, but if you're getting tipsy, agree to stop writing for the evening. Your thank-you notes shouldn't start with the word "Dude!" or end with "I love you, man!"

- Then, collect your list of names and gifts and take a moment to scan through it together, taking the time to think "Wow, we are so lucky to have been treated so well by all of these people!" Now's the time for your verbal celebration, even if you've chatted about this before. How amazing was it for your friend whose wife was expecting twins around the time of your wedding to fly in for the day, even with such a huge financial burden ahead of him? Wasn't it wonderful to have four generations at the wedding? How awesome was it to see all of our families dancing together? Focus on the *experience* of these people's presence, not just the presents. You'll feel warm and much-loved, and that's the right mindset for writing thank-you notes.

✤ Accept that your husband might not have a lot of experience writing formal thank-you notes, so he might feel sheepish in asking you for suggestions on what to write. Be the coolest wife ever by not shaming him with "Didn't you ever do this before?!" but instead provide him with some written suggestions. You're turning each note-writing into a reliving of that gift, giving the *giver* a gift of satisfaction in knowing they chose the right present for you.

When you write the very last thank-you note, create your own celebration by enjoying a movie night where you can catch up on a flick or two that you missed during the most hectic months of your wedding season, or choose movies that make you laugh. You both might choose your own favorite movie to share with your spouse. Pop some gourmet popcorn, pour some drinks, get out the Twizzlers or Junior Mints, and enjoy movie night to celebrate the fact that your evening is not booked with thank-you note writing!

Newlyweds say:
"In the past year, we were really too busy for our family and friends, so we're just blown away that everyone attended and gave us such wonderful presents. We're definitely going to make an effort to attend more family parties, send holiday cards, make plans with friends, e-mail them more, and expand our circle with appreciation for these great people we have!"

Your First Pregnancy Celebration

If this is the right time for a pregnancy, you might find yourself planning a special celebratory dinner when the news comes back positive, or mapping out a treasure hunt for your spouse to follow throughout the house and leading him to that pregnancy test with the plus sign on it. You only get this moment once, so find a great way to share the news with your spouse *and* with your families. Some creative ways newlyweds have done so:

- Create a scrapbook of your and your partner's baby pictures, then have the last page read: "Our Baby's Photo."
- Create an iPod playlist with songs featuring the word "baby" or "child" and wait until your partner gets the message.
- Special-order a T-shirt that says, "I'm Going to Be a Mommy" or "Daddy."
- Buy a pair of baby shoes and present them to your partner, wrapped and with a card announcing the great news.
- Just yell it out when your partner comes home. This is not news for an e-mail or a text message!

CHAPTER 7

Your Personal Goals and Achievements

Each of you has a life of your own, and in that life you have goals and dreams, big personal moments you're working hard to achieve. As a married couple, you are each other's biggest supporters and cheerleaders, always there with a pep talk; always the first person they'll call to announce "I did it!" It's a thrill to know that your spouse is proud of you, and to let your spouse know you always had faith in him, so these celebrations are extra meaningful for you both.

Celebrating a Promotion

When you or your spouse get that big promotion at work, the new title, the corner office, the pay raise, or recognition for all the hard work put into the job, it deserves a major celebration that a spouse can and should throw with extra effort. We do, after all, spend so much of our time at work. It's a big part of our identities, not just how we fill our hours. When you cheer for the big achievement, you're saying "I'm proud of what you do in all ways." Home life and work life aren't always separate— we do bring our jobs home with us every day, and we do make sacrifices of family time to climb up that corporate ladder. Any career person who has ever skipped a family party or had to work during the weekend carries a measure of guilt for all the occasions when a spouse had to go solo to a party or delay weekend or vacation plans. At work, we may deal with a lot of unfairness, social politics, difficult coworkers, a mean boss . . . This celebration is the hard-earned perk that means way more than the keys to the executive restroom. Praise from your spouse, hearing "I'm so proud of you," is a reward all its own.

So say those words! Make a big sign to hang on the front door! Address your spouse as Mister Vice President or Madame CEO when they come home the first time after earning that promotion. Make a

"In our house, we always do themed dinners with professional successes. When my husband got a job in Philadelphia, we celebrated with homemade cheesesteaks. When I got my first book contract, he raided the local gourmet market for specialty items that fit the theme of the cookbook."
—Anne Bramley, Cofounder and host of the Eat Feed Podcasts

big deal out of it, because it *is* a big deal. Too many newlyweds let this moment pass with a hug, and then they make the mistake of talking about what they'll do with all that money that will be coming in! Now's not the time to say, "Hey, now we can go to Paris!" Don't spend the money yet. Focus on the person who earned it.

What's your spouse's favorite celebratory meal? Favorite restaurant? Favorite flower? The tried-and-true celebrations definitely have a place here, and you can add in a few extra touches based on the theme of advancement at work:

+ Create a music mix of songs like "Every Little Thing She Does Is Magic" by Sting, "Respect" by Aretha Franklin, or whichever songs express the "you're awesome" message you're feeling right now.
+ Present your spouse with homemade, preprinted business cards bearing his or her name and the new title, saying that you made these weeks ago because you knew the promotion was coming.
+ Make or buy a card to express how proud you are, how much he or she deserves this new position, and how the sky is the limit. . . .
+ Let your spouse know you're turned on by men or women in power, and start your seduction: "Mister President, would you care to join me in the bedroom?"

Landing a Big Account

We're going with a giant cliché here: When you land a big account, it's often called landing "the big fish," so how about celebrating with an amazing sea bass, salmon, or tuna steak dinner, either prepped in your kitchen, sizzled on the grill, or enjoyed out at a lavish restaurant? Propose a toast to the master of the universe who reeled in the big account, praising his or her business smarts, and letting your spouse know just how proud you really are.

We all want validation and appreciation, and this is a wonderful time for you to celebrate a big accomplishment with a big night out, or in, followed by a theme gift to commemorate the occasion: an umbrella for your rainmaker or a sophisticated pen set for inking future big deals. If pens don't suit the occasion, how about the gift of art, such as a framed print or poster by your spouse's favorite artist? A mover and shaker at the office has to upgrade the wall décor, right?

A new briefcase, a new travel tote, or gleaming coffee canister are the accessories of the modern successful executive, so load your spouse up with the accents he or she would love. Dinner's great, but a gift is a keeper. As are you!

Getting an Interview for a New Job

You'll need to make an impression, so the best thing a spouse can do is take you out for a shopping spree—get that one great suit or silk blouse that says, "I'm a success, and you know I'm the most qualified person for the job." What better way to show your support for your partner than by removing the worry about what to wear, as well as fears about making a good impression, with a shopping spree, including shoes and accessories. While you're on the sartorial impression mindset, consider giving your spouse a gift card to the beauty salon for a haircut, manicure, pedicure, or the works. A calming massage could knead away those preinterview nerves, as well. You're getting your spouse ready for a big opportunity by doing your part to show how much confidence you have that the job is his or hers.

You can run through interview questions the night before or ask your spouse if he or she would prefer to lie low the night before. Some people just like to be on their own. They may want to just quietly think out their answers. They love you, but giving them a night of quiet in the house could be the best celebration ever, since it's a completely selfless gift. And you'll be the best spouse ever for offering the mind-clearing space for your spouse to prepare for the big day.

Getting a New Job

The call has just come in. That new job you just interviewed for is yours. After you break the land-speed record to give your two-week's notice at your old job, it's time to celebrate with your spouse. A new start! A fresh opportunity! The end of the soul-crushing suffering you *both* endured as a result of your being so miserable at work! This is a celebration for you both, then. So either of you may plan it . . . or it might even be a surprise party.

If you've just gotten the job, you might want to keep the news to yourself, sneak home, whip up a fabulous meal, open some wine, put on some music, change into something special, and welcome your spouse home with a bit of a surprise party. The same can be done if he just called to say he snagged the coveted spot. You can still sneak home and jump into those thigh-highs, heels, and garter belt. And maybe you'll choose to cook dinner like this when he arrives home. As newlyweds, these kinds of visual surprises are a celebration unto themselves! It's all the more exciting when you leap into his arms and kiss him with congratulations for the new gig.

Now, another step of your celebration: deciding where to go before you start the new job. Many people give their notice at their old place of employment and still have a week or so until the new job starts, so it's vacation time! (Your spouse can put in for a few vacation days *if* his or her work schedule allows for a short break from the office.) Imagine how relaxed you'll be knowing you are free of the past and ready for the next stage of your career. That needs to be celebrated on an island or at a top-notch resort, with tanned waiters bringing you piña coladas by the pool. Even a three-day jaunt to a desirable vacation spot—perhaps a resort that's always been on your wish list—could be the perfect transition getaway and use of your free time.

What happens if the new job requires you to move? A great opportunity a thousand miles away could mean moving far from your family and friends. It might be a big change, and change can be scary.

If your spouse is unhappy in his or her job, your good news can be a message of "See? A great new position can open up at any time!" Your new job can actually motivate your spouse to start sending out some resumés!

But it can also be good, depending on your personal outlook toward the unknown. Does this dampen the celebration any? Do you have mixed feelings—as many newlyweds do—about the great job opportunity vs. the distance from where you are now? Hold off the celebration until you talk through these issues, since you'll both be on a roller coaster of emotions with this big life transition. Popping corks right now could just unnerve your partner, so hold off until you make a clear decision together, talk through the pros and cons, and really feel the enthusiasm of moving to that great place with potential for growth or a lifestyle slowdown you've always wanted to try. Talk over the fantasies you have about the new life you'll lead together. Once you start getting excited about county fairs or Fashion Week, then you can pop that cork and start looking online for a new home in the new town.

Losing Weight

Save the champagne, ice cream, and brownies for another occasion. Stick some candles into a juicy half of a cantaloupe or cut a wedge of watermelon into the shape of a cupcake! By now, your fitness-minded spouse prefers the healthy stuff over the sugary stuff anyway, so when you create a treat celebration in the form of healthy foods, you show your support and creativity at the same time. Newlyweds who offer a donut find themselves accused of being a saboteur (*"Whyyyy don't you want me to lose weight?!"*). This can be the start of a big fight that sends one or both of you running to the refrigerator for solace. So skip the baked goods and go with something exotic and juicy.

While some couples do set up reward systems for each ten pounds lost, such as "at ten pounds lost, I get a massage; at twenty pounds lost, I get a shopping spree at Victoria's Secret; at thirty pounds lost, I get a shopping spree at Ann Taylor," others see this type of system as too much like bribery and not focused enough on the true reasons for losing weight for health and well-being. Why not have both? A new pair of size-6 pants at Ann Taylor would be great for your well-being, right? So it's up to you if you want to establish a preordained reward system with material and experiential prizes, or if you'll choose to *surprise* your fitness-minded partner with rewards along the way. It's not all about the number on the scale or the size on a pair of pants. It could be a reward for skipping dessert while at a family dinner or for not buying chips during a food shopping trip. Your partner might appreciate your celebrating and reinforcing his or her better life skills and willpower triumphs instead of numbers, especially if a plateau has been reached and

"Make sure you understand why your spouse is doing this, so you can support them for the right reasons. Don't argue for your spouse to do it differently—if you think your spouse is endangering him or herself, find an expert, book, or article that will explain the problem, so your spouse doesn't feel you're not supportive. Let the expert be the naysayer, not you."
—Tina Tessina, Ph.D., Author of *Money, Sex, and Kids*

the scale won't budge. Your gift of a new workout outfit or set of hand weights, an exercise DVD, a cute yoga shirt, or new running sneakers shows that you love your spouse for the effort put in, not just how he or she looks. That's a recipe for success. Everyone wants a spouse like this!

Achieving a Big Fitness Goal

"I don't even like to *drive* twenty-six miles!" says one newlywed who stands amazed that his wife ran a full marathon to support Team in Training, raising funds for the Leukemia & Lymphoma Society. When you or your spouse train for months, endure shin splints or sore shoulders, blisters or bruised knees during preparation for a big race, a big match, or a big meet, that effort needs to be rewarded. Hopefully you've been a great spouse all along, with plenty of supportive words and actions as he or she worked toward the big goal, and now's the time for you to celebrate that great victory. Be there at the finish line! You don't know how many runners cross that line with a tinge of sadness because no friends or family are there to see them. Whatever else may be going on that day, it's not as important as supporting your spouse's great goal. So be there at the halfway mark with a giant sign, be there at a rest stop handing out cups of water (if you sign on to volunteer for the race, you become an even greater support for your spouse!), and be there at the finish line with flowers and a hug.

To celebrate the achievement, choose a great commemorative item, such as a photo of your spouse crossing the finish line (many organizations provide these to all of the athletes), professionally framed with the medal or participant's number included in the frame. Get a little plaque engraved with your spouse's time, and if your spouse always talked about beating Oprah's time in the Marine Corps Marathon she ran, or Katie Holmes's time in the New York City Marathon, get *that* engraved as well: "You beat Oprah!" or "You beat Katie!" This shows you were listening, and it's a great keepsake to show the kids someday.

Another gift that a newlywed might give to their spousal Ironman or Ironwoman is a congratulations card that has been signed by *all* of his or her family and friends, even if it took months to mail that thing around the globe! At the finish line, give your spouse this "we knew you could do it!" card for a priceless end to a hard-earned dream come true—or make it a "we know you *can* do it" card presented before the race starts. Who wouldn't get extra oomph from that?

Whatever the fitness goal, whatever the outcome, your celebration is in showing your partner how much you care about his or her big goals, and the dedication, inner strength, and inspiration it took to take this effort on. And that is often best shared directly, as you massage those sore legs and back for your spouse, speaking words of praise and admiration.

Winning the Big Game

Wise newlyweds continue to enjoy group activities, and if your partnership includes playing in or watching league sports, such as softball or flag football, then you can celebrate the big win together. It might be the championship game or just beating that rival team that's always been a challenge. A victory is a victory, and victory is sweet! Here are some fun ways to celebrate the win:

* Take a video of the game and create an edited version for your spouse and his/her teammates. Add ESPN-like titles and music (but don't steal from the network! You can create your own), have a fun friend provide commentary—perhaps in John Madden's voice and mannerisms—and make it a special presentation a few days after the game.
* Take great photos at the game and make them available to everyone on the team by creating an online photo gallery.
* At the game, fill a big cooler with water—and dump it on the coach.

Our First Big Game Victory

The big game was:

_____

The score was:

_____

The big play was:

_____

_____

✢ Share your stories of past sporting milestones, whether you were an athlete or the best player stuck on the sidelines. This big win might have been a major redemption for you!

✢ Frame the score sheet from the game along with a photo of the team or your favorite player. How great you are to be "the cool spouse" to the rest of the team. It makes your partner look good.

- Join the team in a trip to the local sports bar for pitchers of beer and buffalo wings, or suggest a caravan to the local tavern for a round of drinks.
- Reward your star player with tickets to a professional ballgame for the two of you—or include your families, as well. VIP or box seats are optional.
- Ask your spouse to sign a ball for you. How often does he or she get asked for an autograph? It's a playful part of your celebration.
- Revisit the way you celebrated when playing childhood team sports by going to the ice-cream parlor for a cone or to the pizza place for a slice and a soda.
- After the game, it's time for a shower—another opportunity to celebrate together.

Overcoming a Fear

The best spouses support each other through everything, good and bad. And if part of your "bad" is a lifelong fear of flying or driving over bridges or public speaking or snakes, your partner is right there by your side as you work through your phobia. Fears are nothing to laugh at, and everyone has at least one (those who say they don't are probably lying). When you or your spouse show great courage in taking a fear head-on, as a way to expand your horizons or battle your limits, the wonderful partner is right there with a hug, a cheer, an "I knew you could do it."

Whatever fear is challenged and tackled, no matter how much effort it takes, your celebration should be grand and positive. Maybe you'll get that new flyer a travel pillow or a leather passport case for future use, or a blank photo album where you'll put pictures from your future trips taken together, or arrange a weekend getaway anywhere he or she wants to go.

It takes great trust to confide that you are afraid of something, and to invite a spouse into the process of beating it. So reward that huge emotional leap with a note saying how proud you are, how you'll support him or her through anything, how their courage inspires you. And allow your spouse to design the celebration with you. He or she deserves the power to make that decision.

Appearing in a Newspaper or a Magazine

When you or your spouse accomplish something notable and are featured in the newspaper, in a magazine, or in an association or professional journal, that's cause for a celebration!

Celebrate the fun appearance by running out to get copies of that newspaper or magazine, send copies to parents (who never outgrow the thrill of their children's accomplishments), send the link to friends when the material is available online, and if the achievement is a big one, frame it for your partner. That extra effort shows how proud you are, especially when you hang it in your home as a big show of your partner's success. You support each other in all the days and nights of your careers, or in your charity work, so this celebration says "this is not a small deal to me." Your appreciation and validation of your spouse's work is like a long-life tonic to your marriage. It's the fuel that keeps you close. Every time your spouse sees that framed article and remembers your efforts, it'll feel wonderful.

Passing a Big Exam

Passing the bar or a medical board, even a final exam or dissertation is a big deal. A very big deal. And a supportive spouse makes it a big deal at home. Throw a party or plan a special dinner or a weekend getaway. If your spouse was fully absorbed for months in studying for the exam, if he or she missed out on social events, this is a big welcome back to regular life and to your partnership. So make a big sign to hang in the house, a colorful banner that you can make by hand or have printed up at a sign store or copy shop. Fill the living room with balloons. Get an ice-cream cake. Pop a cork on some champagne. Do a silly little congratulations dance, the sillier the better as a cute little gift to your spouse. (Come on, you know you have a Happy Dance that you do when things go well, so break out that Cabbage Patch move from the 80s!). Invite friends, especially if your spouse has been a bit of a hermit while studying.

Shower your partner with theme gifts, too: perhaps a leather briefcase for your new attorney; or a selection of great, colorful nurse's shirts for your new RN; a gift card to a stationery shop where your spouse can design his or her new business cards; an engraved plaque for a desk that follows his or her name with Ph.D., Esquire, or other achievement. How about a tie with the little medical emblem on it? Or any variation of alumni goodies bought at the school store, such as a mug that says "Harvard Law" on it? Your spouse might not have purchased these keepers for himself, so they could be a perfect gift now.

And as for a verbal celebration, tell your spouse if you prayed for a passing grade, if you lit good luck candles, or forwarded a chain letter for the first time in your life because you didn't want to jinx their test results. These superstitions and faith actions will mean a lot to your partner, even if they're a little bit wacky—*especially* if they're a little bit wacky. You're a supportive spouse, and you're not afraid to show what you think will bring luck. "I feng shui'd the Success corner of the house" might get a chuckle, but aren't you cute for putting a little mirror on the mantel because you thought there was a chance it would help? And hey, it just might have worked!

This is a big accomplishment that deserves a congratulations card that will be kept forever: This moment in time should be commemorated by great photos or video of your spouse opening that letter on the day the test results finally arrived in the mail. Frame that letter! Add a page to your family scrapbook with this big achievement noted and preserved for all time. It's a big shift in your life together when either of you makes such a big transition, and this is the start of a whole new future for you both. Now *that* deserves a celebration!

Having a Difficult Personal Conversation with a Parent, Sibling, or Friend

You've known for a long time that you have to confront a relative or friend about something tough, but you never had the right words or the courage to confront them about a substance problem, your concerns about their health, or their bad relationship, even a parent's bad behavior toward your spouse. Most people would rather avoid a confrontation, but it's gotten to the point where you have to sit them down and talk to them. You've spent time prepping, maybe reading a book or talking with a therapist to learn how to say things the right way, and you've stressed out for many a night trying to figure out how to solve the problem.

You just couldn't let things continue as they were. A good friend, a good sibling, a good son or daughter, a good spouse finds it within themselves to risk a loved one's anger in order to say what needs to be said, because not speaking up could contribute to disaster. You love that person enough to put yourself at risk for an argument or hurt feelings. It can be truly terrifying.

With pulse pounding, you did it. You told your sister that she should leave her abusive boyfriend. You've told your father he needs to get treatment for alcoholism. You've told your mother that any disrespect shown to your spouse is disrespect shown to *you*. You said all you needed to say, expressed your love and support, maybe heard a few insults from their reared-up defense mechanisms. You went through the fire for them.

The next step is up to them. You did your part as a loved one, and if it's your spouse who did the confronting and delivered the tough love, your celebration is one of a more serious nature. No one's breaking out the party hats. This is a hug at the kitchen counter as your spouse breaks down in tears over how emotional that was, how tough it was to see the hurt in their father's eyes, how worried she still is that her sister won't leave an abusive relationship. This is a moment when you connect and share your strength with your partner, or your partner with you. The celebration may be a silent one, a message of "I am with you in this, no matter what comes of it." It's telling your spouse how brave he is, how so many people don't have the courage to say something.

Your celebration is in unconditional support and your availability to help in any way when the loved one does take action. Maybe you'll offer to take the sister's dogs while she and the kids go to a safe house. Maybe you'll offer to work for free at the father's office while he's in rehab. Maybe you'll offer to forgive the mother for the unkind treatment she's given you, give her a blank slate for the future. These would all be tremendous gifts to your spouse. What you offer right now is the true celebration.

Your First Pep Talk

Everybody has a bad day from time to time, and it's so wonderful to come home to your spouse for a bit of comforting. Having your best friend right there to cheer you up and give you a pep talk when you need one is one of the perks of being married, right? You've often consoled each other and given each other a boost on blue days, but this is your first major pep talk as husband and wife. So if your spouse needs an uplifting conversation, make sure you provide an extra measure of pampering, such as a back rub, or introduce a new tradition of a great foot rub whenever either of you need it. Announcing, "Honey, I had a crappy day" can soon be your message that it's time to get out the good foot lotion, that coconut-and-honey-scented brand you love, and bring your spouse to the couch, take off those shoes and socks, and work your magic on your partner's aching feet. With so many reflexology points on the foot, you'll easily calm your partner's entire being.

As you pamper your spouse, you can deliver the most encouraging and calming message of love, and your celebration is just having this person in your life to comfort, and having the right words to bring a smile to that face again. You have so much power to lift your partner's spirits—sometimes just the sound of your voice, or being there together, getting this one-on-one time, is a celebration all on its own.

And if this is a soul-cleansing crying session, just let the tears flow, hand over those aloe-infused tissues, and don't judge and don't try to solve the problem with a simplistic piece of advice. This isn't a sitcom.

> **GUYS' TIP**
>
> Some problems can't be solved in a half hour. Sometimes you just have to let your partner cry it out, releasing that frustration and being safe with you to vent. What she might need most is to just sob and gurgle out unintelligible things into your shoulder. That's what best friends are for.

The First Business Trip

You're not celebrating the fact that one of you is going on a long business trip, putting lots of miles between the two of you. You're celebrating the fact that you can be apart for a measure of time without it being the end of the world. In any good marriage, there's a healthy space between two partners. It's when a spouse doesn't have friends, a social life, interests, or the ability to go a day without speaking to or seeing a partner that problems happen. That's when you're too clingy and dependent, smothering and needy. No one wants a spouse like that, and unhealthy dependency has split plenty of couples up.

So while your spouse is away, sure you can talk on the phone each night—but don't call twenty times a day and don't interrogate her about who she may have had dinner with. Don't cry and get hysterical, and don't call him for little "rescues," such as "the power went out, so how do I fix the clock?" It's a danger to your relationship if either of you plays the helpless card—or the jealousy card.

Instead, turn this time apart—a time when a business trip could mean a big deal or a big promotion, a new account and good standing with the company—into a celebration of how confident you are, how self-sufficient, how social, how capable you are. Yes, it's sweet to say, "I miss you." You just don't want to be a blubbering wreck when you say that. Your spouse will celebrate being married to such a complete person, and you can celebrate being married to such a complete person, as well, if your partner behaves the same self-confident way toward you back at home!

Each day, you celebrate your independence in a good way, with lots of activities, such as going to see a museum exhibit or running in the park. These things make you more interesting. That's way better than guilting your partner for going away and having fun at a resort while you watched television and took out the garbage (insert giant *sigh* here).

Now, with the duration of the trip covered by your super-cool behavior and your sweet messages of love during your evening or morning chats, it's time to plan the celebration of your spouse's first time *coming home*! Prepare a great meal with a formally set table, and light candles. Shower and change into an alluring outfit. That's way better than being in sweats and a ponytail when he walks in the door, or in sweaty workout clothes when she wheels her suitcases into the garage. Dress up and make this celebration a grand one. Or if you are the one coming home, make sure you bring a little something for your partner to show how much you missed them and appreciated their support while you were away.

Don't expect sex this night, but be ready for it. A day of travel may have exhausted your partner, or she might be raring to go the minute she walks in the door. Better to be shaved and coiffed and ready if your spouse is. But your spouse may prefer to cuddle on the couch instead of working on that "Around the World" list you have going on. This might have been a hectic week of meetings and travel, and the best welcome home celebration may just be *not* having *anything* to do.

♥

PART TWO

Overcoming the First Challenges Together

CHAPTER 8

The Business Side of Life

Not everything is going to be rosy during your first year together. After the fairy tale of the wedding is over, reality can come crashing down—especially financial reality. Every newlywed encounters this, so here are some of the challenges you may face together, and ways to cope so you can find solutions together. Remember: Challenges are a gift. They get you communicating. Even in an argument, you can hear your spouse's deepest truths. That's the work of a good marriage. You promised to face the future together.

YOUR "FINANCIAL SUMMIT"

You've talked about the basics of creating a budget together, so you know what it takes to invite your spouse to discuss your finances, and you know that basic budget was relatively simple to create. Now you're proposing a much bigger topic: "We have to talk about our finances, debts, savings, investments, and emergency fund." Yikes! Those are heavy, serious topics, and *both* of you have to be in the mood to focus on your financial plan, share ideas equally, compromise, and—most importantly—be open to trying your spouse's method of dealing with money issues. You're meeting in the middle at this Financial Summit, working through as much resistance or challenges as possible toward organizational plans and rules on the topics of:

* Checking
* Savings
* Emergency fund amount (is three months' salary enough?)
* Credit card debt
* School loans
* Car payments
* Your credit reports, credit scores, and FICO score (visit www.myfico.com)
* Expendable cash
* Adjustments to your budget
* Any loans that you're considering

Remember: You're full partners with your money, so share decisions before you buy or invest. This summit gets you both on the same page with your finances.

The First Fight Over Wedding Expenses

Well, you thought you'd get enough money in cash wedding gifts from your guests in order to cover what you spent on the wedding (actually, you thought you'd turn a profit!). But that didn't happen. Now, with the wedding over, the credit card bills are rolling in, and you owe *a lot*. This is when many newlyweds have their first big money fight . . . and as with all money fights, it's not really just about the actual dollar amount; it's often about much deeper things, like self-control, a sense of entitlement, a perceived irresponsibility. You and your partner might be simmering with these kinds of negative thoughts about each other, and now it looks like someone has made a mess with the family finances! "You *had* to have a designer gown!" or "You just *had* to have a bigger wedding than your sister!" or "I *told* you we couldn't afford the limo!" are common battle cries and verbal assaults on partners after a wedding. You had your dream day, but now the debt is a nightmare.

Money problems are a top stressor for couples, so you have to have a plan for dealing with the debt crush that may follow your wedding. Your first step in dealing with the money hangover is to expect that you'll have debt. Don't set yourself up for a miserable first few months of marriage with the irrational expectation that you'll make money on the wedding. If you expect to take a financial hit, it will hurt less.

Next, talk right now about your shared happiness about every plan you made. Watch the wedding video, if you have it, to see the smiles on your faces—and on your families' faces. Discuss the fact that this was much more than a wedding—it was a milestone event for the family, a priceless point in time where your parents are healthy and dancing with you, friends have flown in from around the world to be with you, and your vows hold so much meaning. You have to redefine what that money bought you. That way, it's not just about the topical expense of a dress, a cake, a limo, and flowers. Those were accents to a much, much bigger day of great meaning.

It was your day, and you're willing to tighten the belt for a while after the wedding to catch up on the debt from it.

Now, you must refrain from blaming your partner for any decisions or plans made for the day. If she gave into a florist who wanted to expand on your vision for "just $2,000 more," don't give her a hard time now. Yes, it may have been a mistake to order that many orchids or the flowering trees for the ballroom, but what's done is done. It was gorgeous at the time, so there's no need to throw mud on the memory because of dollar amounts. If you avoid shaming your partner, you avoid adding guilt and resentment to the big bucket of problems you have here. No one likes being lectured or talked down to. You promised to love, honor, and cherish in good times and in bad. Well, you've just hit a bit of a bad time, so keep your word. Your loved one may have messed up, and the question now is "What are we going to do about it?" The key word being *we*. It's not fair to make your partner scrimp and save to pay for those flowers, while you're enjoying your own money without a care in the world. This is your shared debt, so don't play parent by punishing your partner financially for what went into the wedding that you, too, enjoyed. Emotional warfare will erode your marriage, so this is a good lesson for you both: accept your partner's flaws in every area, including financial responsibility, and proceed from here with a solid pay-off-the-debt plan.

Again, you didn't *waste* money on the wedding. One partner saying that hurts the other partner's feelings. You just attacked her dream, and will she have trust in you to protect her future dreams? And what about her support for your dreams? Think about it.

The First Fight About Credit Card Debt

We're talking existing credit card debt that you might bring into the marriage. The bigger issue here—no matter what your balances are—is whether or not you were honest and open with your partner about the amount you owe, if you had late payments, or if you have a bad credit rating. Did you hide your credit card bills when they arrived in the mail, so she wouldn't see the balances? Deceit and secrets are not the foundation of a strong marriage, especially when it comes to money. Newlyweds have been known to split up because one kept big financial secrets from the other.

If you have high balances and haven't told your partner, enact your payoff plan now. Cut up those high-balance cards and create a realistic payback plan. So when you *do* talk to your partner about your credit card debt, you can show that you've already taken steps to remedy the less-than-wise spending habits you've had. Show your planned monthly payments to get those balances down, talk about how you've been brown-bagging your lunches at work and saving hundreds per month. It's important to show *quantifiable* steps and results that your partner can grasp. That works much better than simply saying "I'm going to stop getting manicures." If you preempt the fight, and if you can show smart financial efforts in the interest of making your marriage strong, it's going to help cushion the blow when you do reveal your financial situation to your spouse.

If debt is discovered by a spouse, especially if it's in an embarrassing way—like if you're applying for a mortgage together and the loan officer tells your spouse about your debts and bad credit rating (Ouch! Hurt + humiliation = anger)—you might just have a big fight on your hands. And "I didn't want you to be mad" as a reason for not sharing the secret is really code for "I didn't want to face up to how mad you were going to be."

The secretive spouse will get a much worse "mark" than a bad credit rating. He might permanently damage his spouse's trust level in him. "If you kept a secret about this, what else have you kept secret?" It's a downward spiral that's a cancer to any marriage.

Trust is essential to a partnership, and trust with money is also essential.

So when the storm breaks, your apologies may fall on deaf ears at first, but your only recourse is to be fully willing to change your financial

"It's not so much that she had high credit card bills, but that she hid it from me. All I can think of now is that she did a lot of things, took a lot of secretive steps, to keep this from me all this time. *That's what I'm upset about.* That, and finding out *after* the wedding. I feel very betrayed by the hiding of it, not the debt itself."

—David, A newlywed from San Francisco

ways, pay back your debts as an investment *in your marriage,* and start on that long road earning back your partner's trust. Changing money habits may seem difficult at first, but it's just like dieting. A little bit of sacrifice and self-control shows results in just a short period of time, and then you're much healthier to live a longer and more satisfying financial life. That's what you owe your spouse, so vow to never keep financial secrets again.

The First Fight About Spending vs. Saving

We all grow up with different money styles. Some people are spenders and some are savers—and some are a combination of the two. When you and your spouse fell in love, you may have noticed your differences or similarities with regard to your relationship to money, but it's never mattered more than now. As a married couple, your patterns of spending or saving affect *both* of you. It *is* your partner's business how you handle money, just as it is your business how your partner handles money. So when you have your first clash over spending vs. saving, know that this powerful dynamic is coming into focus, but it's been there all along.

The first blowout over how you direct your money is likely to be a very emotionally charged one, especially if you're only recently living together and merging your financial efforts for the first time. Conflict skills are a part of this issue as well. How does your partner speak to you when he's upset? How does your partner direct your efforts: as requests or as demands? Do you feel like a little girl with a disapproving parent standing over you when your husband questions how much you're putting into savings, or how little money you have left over at the end of a pay cycle?

In this first fight, it is possible that both of you will do everything wrong, so be ready for that. It may be an ugly encounter, but keep this in mind: *this is an important fight, because when the dust settles, you'll both be able to adjust your attitudes and conflict skills for the next time.* And there will be a next time. Every couple has fights about money. If yours turns into a gruesome argument where hurtful things are said or the silent treatment is given, you're not alone. Remember that you're not going to get it right this first time. So after the insensitive things have been said, you've both retreated to separate rooms, stewed for a while, reviewed the conversation in your heads a few hundred times to think about what *each* of you did wrong, you can come together in peace and apologize, and soon after discuss what you need from each other, and what you don't want to experience again.

Almost all fights about money revolve around how the other person made you feel. That's what you remember for a long time, so keep that in mind when you're talking to your spouse. You don't want to be the big problem here.

"Please don't say that I throw my money away on dumb things," might be expressed in the debriefing stage of this argument. "My father always said that to me when I was growing up, and the message I got was that I didn't deserve anything nice in my life. So when you take that same tone, I feel like you're talking down to me and hitting that same nerve." You're letting your partner know what's fair and what's unacceptable to say to you. A wise newlywed does this *now*, letting their partner into their thinking and their deeper issues.

It's not going to take just one fight to turn you into a saver if that's not your longtime pattern, so explain to your spouse that you respect the request and agree to have an emergency fund or put more into a retirement account. So open up a savings plan, and put 10% of your paycheck into it. But you're not necessarily going to have to put *all* of your leftover money into savings, because it's also important for you to keep some of your own indulgences. You'd feel deprived if you didn't have some form of retail fun. And if your spouse is the spender who enjoys spending recreationally, you can offer the same type of plan: "How about if we both put 5% of our paychecks into an emergency fund?" might be well-received. A minor shift can lead to major gains down the road, and you both compromise your ways in the healthier "moving toward the middle" partnership of marriage.

This fight then becomes a *good* thing, opening the door to a calm, rational discussion and a new plan that makes you both more relieved. After apologies, you grow closer.

The First Time Money Secrets Are Revealed

You had no idea he was giving his brother money. He had no idea you had $50,000 in student loans. We've already discussed the importance of financial honesty when it comes to credit card debt, so read back over the important steps in the big reveal of your financial burdens. What we're talking about here are different types of debts, the kinds that "just never came up" in conversation. And in this first fight when you see a $3,000 check made out to his brother, especially hurtful when you're living month to month, you'll likely stumble upon one of those newlywed mistakes: He didn't want to tell you because you would have said no. And you would have called his brother a loser. And he would have had to give the money against your wishes. And you would have had a fight.

And he's right. Would you have said, "Oh, sure! Give your brother a few grand so that he can take his garage band on the road and become famous. I'm more than happy to pay the electric, gas, and water bills while you nurture his dreams!" Nah, you'd have gotten mad. The truth is, we all have responsibilities and guilt-trip buttons with our families, and we may feel compelled to help them out, even when all logic says not to. And if the secret is your gigantic student loan bill, you did what you thought was best to avoid a confrontation. "It just didn't come up . . ."

Now that it has come up, the best thing you can do as newlyweds is to back off and not fight about a decision either of you made in the past with the intention of peace and harmony between you. Remember: Neither one of you should feel entitled to make all the financial decisions in the family. Yes, it was crummy of him to sneak that $3,000 out of the checking account, but do you really want a marriage where either of you is the boss when it comes to money, with every check needing to be cleared by you—or by your spouse—first? This first big argument about secret payments (unless they're to a brothel or a loan shark) allows you to give your partner a break this time. By being safe to talk to, you'll show that you are open to such conversations and start a conversation about truth and honesty in all financial dealings. This is where you might remind each other that you have separate accounts of your own spending money, and neither of you has to ask permission for purchases and the like. But you can't have a situation where you're scraping up the money to pay the electric bill, and he's indulging his brother's latest whim. "Let's create a new bill-payment plan, because this isn't working" means that this secret check to his brother just turned into a positive money discussion for you, where your household bills will be more evenly split in the future.

He may always want to give his brother money, if it's been his longtime pattern to take care of his little bro who's just trying to "find himself." You may see it as wrong, but he has to make the decision to stop on his own, and he may do so if you gently say, "Your brother has to learn how to make money realistically." Plus, in the future, you're both likely to be helping out your parents financially. The money in your hands isn't always going to be yours as a couple, so now is when you talk out the plans for when others need your help. Little bro just did you a big favor.

This first fight sure brought up some great topics to discuss for your financial plan, didn't it?

The bottom line: You don't have to keep money secrets from each other. It's a sign of great love and trust that you'll talk to each other, and feel safe doing it because you both respect the other's right not to be kept in the dark. The secret, again, is the relationship-killer. You can both acknowledge that.

The First Conflict Over Household Money and Bills

What happens when it's your first time facing shared household expenses, like a mortgage or rent, the electric or gas bill, cable, groceries, etc.? Again, if you've lived together for a while, you might have worked out a system where you both pay your chosen utility bills, and then you meet up in a few months to tally who paid what and even out the difference. That's the plan in a perfect world.

If you're new to living together, you might run into a newlywed mistake of wanting to just be agreeable. *I'll take on the gas and electric, and you pay the phone and Internet.* Months later, you're paying thousands and your partner is paying hundreds. And you're too nervous to say, "Hey, can you give me $1,000 since I'm paying so much more for my share of the bills?" If only we could all be so assertive and direct! But not all couples can do this right away. It's one of those beginner lessons that every newlywed faces. After this first conflict, you should work out a plan to match the one mentioned at the start of this section.

Money is a loaded issue for couples. It's one of the top causes of fights. We're all wired with different fears and habits when it comes to our money. Some spend, some save. Some pay the bills as soon as they come in, and some wait until right before the due date (which might drive the other partner crazy). Some don't open the mail and bills might even be missed and paid late (gulp!).

Money blowouts often happen a few months into the marriage if you haven't already sat down for a Money Summit. If both partners want to be agreeable, or avoid the bills because they don't want to fight or hurt the other's feelings, this invites conflict. And conflict can be good. Because this first money fight is going to clear the air, get the issues on the table, and educate each of you about the other's money habits. It's an unpleasant way to get there, since money fights can end with slammed doors and the dreaded litany of all the shoes you bought last summer. But consider it like the sting of hydrogen peroxide on a fresh cut. It hurts, but it has to clean the wound.

The blowout just shows you that you need to sit down and talk. *Now.*

Spread out the utility bills and the cable bills, the food shopping receipts and everything else that's eaten at both of your bank accounts, and make a list of who paid for what. Here's where you talk about the fact that the gas bill is going to be insanely high during the winter, so your spouse can take over the dry cleaning bills during the winter to even things out. Reiterate that all expenses need to be divided evenly to keep things fair—especially if one of you earns more money than the other.

Here's your script: "I know it's uncomfortable to talk about money, but I don't want either of us to simmer and blow up over our chosen bills. So let's get ahead of the issue by drawing up a budget which we can play with over time." Never assume that your partner is enjoying the fact that you have all the big bills to pay. That's an unfair accusation to make, unless he's a big jackass and has actually said that to you. In which case, you might need to talk to a marriage counselor.

Yes, the first money fight is a given, and it's going to happen. It's only a matter of time. What matters most is how you handle the challenge, how you promise each other to live "in good times and in bad; for richer and for poorer." Remember those? The best plan for newlyweds is to agree to try different financial arrangements, adjusting over time, and meeting every few months to even up funds. That shows great equality in a marriage. It also shows that you value each other.

And when you assure each other that you have one another's back when you're short on cash, you've just grown closer and done the great work of the first year of marriage.

A few other things to discuss with your spouse:

- You won't talk about your household finances with others.
- You won't shame the other for having low funds or for missing a payment due to disorganization.
- You won't hide your purchases, since honesty is a bedrock of a healthy marriage.
- You'll establish both a Fun Fund and an Emergency Fund to give your marriage a level of security that removes big money stress.
- You'll both keep your individual accounts and credit cards, and then create a new joint account for shared bills.
- You'll both promise to consider adjusting to each other's bill-paying style. Maybe his practice of paying at the last minute can be adjusted to paying a little bit earlier, as a kindness to you in preventing your stressing over it.
- You'll both agree that it'll take some time for you to adjust to the new agreements, and that backsliding is okay with communication and gentle correction.
- You'll invest in a smart money-management book so that you can work together to achieve your financial goals.

The First Conflict Over the Difference in Your Income Levels

If one of you makes more money than the other, you've probably been living with that difference for quite a while. Now that you're married, it can become a conflict when it comes down to dividing the household bills evenly, paying a mortgage or rent that's more of a struggle for one of you than the other, and having disposable income without an equitable plan. This conflict often starts to grow quietly and then surfaces at bill-paying time or when one of you makes a simple comment about the household expenses, such as "Well, I'm not *rich* like you are!" or "Hey, I work just as hard as you do!" Yes, these comebacks can be juvenile; they come from a place of frustration. This can really surprise a partner who had no idea the income level discrepancy was ever an issue. So that can lead to an icy comeback, a self-defense of "I provide well for us!" which is then heard with a tacked-on, *not like you*. It just gets nastier from there.

The first fight over income discrepancy may hit at the very core of you. If you're the moneyed one, you might think *don't guilt-trip me for being successful.* If you're the one earning less, or perhaps unemployed or staying home with kids, you might be trying to bring your partner down to size because you feel insecure. Money frustrations can bring out the worst in us, even if we're dealing with someone we love very much. Newlyweds often have a hard time getting this topic out in the open. The conflict might start off as little jokes, snide comments, or passive-aggressive actions. But those are just the preludes to the big fight.

It's important to realize that you're not fighting over what's on your W2s at the end of the year. You're fighting because one of you has abundance, and one of you doesn't. Not every spouse is mature about this. Some may feel that because they have the higher-paying job, their partner should do more of the housework. Pretty soon, that spouse has stopped going with you to do the food shopping. This difference in income turns into a difference in status in the home. You have to stop this virus from eating away at your relationship, or else a big divide is going to grow between you. One of you will become the boss and the other will become the subordinate. It happens gradually in marriages, and anything that separates spouses needs to be quashed immediately.

So when the fight breaks out, it's just a big spotlight on the issue that's there. The unspoken truth is: *Neither of us is more important than the other because of what we make. We're equals, and we need to reinstate the equality in our marriage.*

That's going to take an attitude adjustment and great honesty on both of your parts. Because your partner might not be a rich jerk who treats you like a subordinate, but you might be *interpreting* his working late while you do the scheduled food shopping as his doing something wrong. Your spouse is just at work. He hasn't announced, "I'm no longer doing the food shopping because I make $30,000 more than you." You might have grabbed this one incident and loaded your growing resentment onto it. So that's why you need to have this fight—to get those frustrations out, hear him tell you you're making too much of it (he might be right), have him hear you say you don't want the housework to fall on you (you might be right), and then when the dust settles, you can talk over the shifts you need to make to gain back that equality, the appreciation you need, and the new payment plan that would make bill-paying more fair.

And then both of you should thank the other for all of your hard work in every area of your lives, showing appreciation for the great life that's been made possible by both of your contributions. Even if it's just a hug and a simple sentence, it's something that millions of couples would give a kidney to hear from their spouses.

"Unless each of you have exactly the same job, it is nearly impossible to think you'll be at the same exact income level. You also want to stop thinking about income as simply the size of a paycheck, and instead, think of the total compensation. This means you should take into account various insurance benefits, vacation time, retirement plans, and so on. What you'll often find is that while one person's actual net income might be lower, they may actually be receiving other benefits that don't directly translate into a dollar amount."

—Jeremy Vohwinkle, Financial Planning Guide at About.com

The First Time You Bail Out
Your Partner Financially

You're partners in all things, and you would do anything to protect your spouse from harm, so when your spouse falls into a big financial problem and needs extra cash, you're more than happy to step in with a blank check and a hug. Right? Of course you are. You vowed *for richer or for poorer* at the wedding, and you meant it. But the challenge arises when a darker mindset creeps into this money rescue. The person giving the money is the hero, and the person needing the money is needy. Whenever you have these disparate, emotionally loaded roles going on in a relationship, they're like poison. So you must prevent those characterizations from ever taking root. Just rip them right out of the ground whenever they start to sprout.

That means establishing some rules about *any* money given to one another—and smart newlyweds talk about this *now* before anything is ever handed over:

* You will establish whether the money is a loan or a gift. Put it in writing either way. Yes, this seems very *People's Court* with hastily written agreements on cocktail napkins, but this isn't a matter of not trusting your partner. It's more a matter of getting the issue out of your head and onto paper. It's a protective thing. By writing it down, you have it in clear terms that this is a *gift*, not a loan to be paid back in a few months. You both must be clear on the terms—super clear, because having different expectations on a payback plan is going to simmer into resentment and anger.

* If it's a loan, you'll agree to pay installments on time every time. This is an expression of your integrity.

* Do it legally. Ask a financial advisor for advice on how you'll both record the transaction in your records. Are gifts to a spouse below a certain amount tax-free in your state? Get the facts.

* Never, ever remind your partner that you gave or lent them money. This is not something to be used as a weapon in the future, such as

when you're arguing about spending habits. Spitting out "At least I can pay my bills!" is the verbal equivalent of hitting your spouse over the head with a board. That kind of comment can stay with a person forever.

※ Don't tell a soul about your spouse needing money. Some might think that gossip is harmless, and some might want to look admirable to others. "I just lent my wife $5,000" makes you sound like a big shot, but this transaction between the two of you should stay between the two of you. Gossip always gets back to the person being spoken about, and that's a terrible betrayal of trust.

✛ Have empathy for your spouse's situation. Yes, you may see that he didn't make smart choices on the path that led him to need money from you, but now's not the time to lecture, scold, instruct, or shame. It's very hard to ask for and accept money from your spouse. Just provide the help without judgment.

✛ Know how to suggest help for your spouse. If this is a matter of compulsive spending, gambling, or addiction, you *can* stipulate that your spouse seek professional help from a therapist or recovery group. After any initial resistance, you can explain that you'll support him or her in all ways so that will prevent future financial problems. You won't always be able to bail him or her out. It's tough to put a condition on a financial bailout, but consider it an investment in your spouse's health, your health, and the health of the marriage. You simply can't turn into an ATM or a doormat. You're lovingly pointing your spouse toward the help that an adult needs to be willing to accept, or at least try, as the give-and-take of marriage. It can't be all take, or you won't last very long.

CHAPTER 9

Combining Your Home Well

Setting up your home together involves way more than just arranging couches and chairs to create a good traffic pattern, or hanging pictures on the walls. For some couples who haven't lived together before marriage, conflicts arise about whose belongings are *more important*—at least that's how it can feel as you're in the process of deciding which items to keep and which to toss. "Why your couch and not mine?" and "We're not putting all of my dishes in the attic while we only use yours" and "What about *my* comforter for the bed?" There's an awful lot of measuring that goes on as couples try to keep a balance between *yours, mine,* and *ours,* and when that balance gets thrown off, one partner can feel left out or that their partner is taking over the house, while they're expected to throw out or donate the items they love. It can become territorial. And when that conflict hits, the entire process of setting up your home becomes a smashed illusion, a broken dream—when it can be really fun.

Another tough part of combining items into a unified home is the feeling that your taste is not appreciated. When one partner takes on the role of interior decorator, there's that discrepancy again—you're not equals. And a home requires the partnership of equals. So in this section, we'll tackle the conflicts that often arise when newlyweds combine their favorite belongings, their furniture, their artwork, their pasts into their new, shared world.

The First Conflict Over Whose Belongings Stay or Go

Make it clear from the start: No "rejection" of your belongings is a rejection of *you.* The only way to move forward into this task is with an agreement that requests or choices are not any kind of judgment on taste, and that no one is trying to "take over" the house. These things need to be said out loud to remove either of your sensitivities during this emotionally charged work you're doing. Yes, it's fun and exciting to set up your home together. But it's also daunting to select from your belongings, especially when you have many duplicates.

And this brings up another tip: Don't agree to give up your stuff just to be agreeable or to fit some kind of fairy-tale image of your role in this task, because you will regret it, and then resent your partner for what your mind rewrites into a vision of "he made me give up my stuff." Be willing to say "no." Good partners can hear that from each other and be okay with it.

As a good rule of thumb, agree to set out the chosen pieces, and then store the duplicates away. Don't call the donation truck right away. Give yourselves a few months to live with your choices, see how they work for you, and then consider switching some items for the things in the basement. If you know your things are still with you, it can be easier to progress with this first step of combining your belongings.

Some couples make an actual chart of what stays and what goes, using columns to be sure there's an equal give-and-take between partners. It might be easier for you to see it in writing that, yes, he has given up his chair, his entertainment center, and his bedding to accommodate your items. A frazzled mind can evade reality and paint a gloomy picture of extremes. It may feel like he has more of his stuff being used, but it's really quite even.

If you're truly embattled about a specific chair for the living room, use it in another place in the house, such as a home office or the second bedroom, a refinished basement or the dining room. You can repurpose your belongings, too!

When you fight about your stuff, in many cases you're clinging to the life you led before marriage. Getting rid of anything can definitely feel like a loss—of the piece and of memories associated with it. But you have to accept that creating a new home together means you will *both* lose things, just as you both will gain far more in this new home you're creating together.

The First Conflict About Clutter

One of you may be quite comfortable with clutter, while the other may feel suffocated, overwhelmed by the pile of catalogs, unopened mail, shopping bags with receipts in them, and other things covering the dining room table. We each have a threshold on the amount of chaos we can handle in our environment, whether or not you believe in feng shui. A cluttered home can make you feel jittery, tired, unmotivated, and out of control.

So when you clash over the mail on the counter, when your spouse doesn't put his unopened mail in the bin you specifically set out and labeled, know that you're dealing with something bigger than a pile of junk mail: You're likely dealing with a control issue, too. Maybe your spouse doesn't want to be told how to arrange the mail.

You're both just starting out in a new life together, so you have to corral any control issues that float between you, starting with skirmishes over the amount of clutter in the house. Be direct. "Honey, I grew up in a very messy house, and it was always tough for me to come home from college and enter my parents' place where there wasn't a clean surface anywhere. It really affected me then, and I don't want to live in a cluttered home now." You've explained your issue with the clutter. "So can we agree to put the unopened mail in this bin, just to keep it out of the way? I'm not saying you have to go through your mail every day. Let's just keep it all in one place, instead of in three rooms." You're calmly and respectfully asking, not demanding, which is what your partner will learn to do when he has a change he wants to make to *your* longtime patterns.

Give it a while to sink in. It might take a few tries before he stops dropping mail everywhere. Longtime patterns take a long time to break. When he does put the clutter away, give plenty of positive reinforcement, including a thank you or a back rub. But remember, this is not a child you're "training," so don't go overboard with the praise. The guy put an envelope in a bin. He didn't win the Nobel Peace Prize. How insulted would you be if you were over-praised and spoken to like a puppy.

Make a plan for straightening up, such as every Sunday night, you'll both take a pass through the house to get rid of clutter and empty

"Rather than having a heated argument about clutter [with my husband], I have often just taken the bull by the horns and entered the mess with gusto, sorting through piles of unwanted and accumulated excess. My husband—after seeing how things were shaping up, decided to help out and was soon inspired by the improvement, thanking me and joining in to help make the process easier."

—Kim Parker, Author of *Kim Parker Home*

the trash cans. Just ten minutes of effort, that will soon become your Sunday night ritual. Especially if you follow it up with a great dinner. Some couples establish Sunday night pasta dinners, and they reward themselves with this cozy, job-well-done meal after they each tackle a few items on the to-do list, including getting rid of clutter.

You have to understand that clutter can have a numbing effect on your partner, making them even less likely to start cleaning, just as you may be drained by the chaos of clutter. Spouses are not mind-readers. Don't make the newlywed mistake of slapping on a smile and trying to adjust to it. The sooner you're direct about the problem, the better.

He'll figure out that you're happier in a clutter-free home, and when you're happy, he's happy. It's a win-win.

The First Conflict About Decorating Your Home

Who knew you could get into such a big fight about *curtains?* Why does he have such strong feelings about your wispy beige sheers, anyway? Well, you might have brushed up against a wound he has. He doesn't want anyone telling him what to do. He may have a long history of parents and exes replacing his plans or overruling him on his wishes, and these curtains were just the last straw.

Most newlywed fights have their roots in longtime wounds, and with you two so close, you're bound to tweak a few of them, innocently and without malice. But it does hurt your partner nonetheless. So when he freaks out over your curtain choices, especially if you hung them when he was out of the house, you're not fighting about the curtains. You're fighting because you just did what someone else did a long time ago, something that he never got over.

So what are you supposed to do? After you fight it out a little bit (which can be cathartic), go for the solution. "Okay, you didn't like it that I put the curtains up without you. From now on, neither of us will do anything to the house without the other sharing in the fun." You

> **Make it a rule that one partner's "no" is a final decision. Neither of you should have to live with a style you hate.**

just ended your sentence with a positive statement, not the dreaded "without the other's permission," because that's too parental. (That may be *exactly* where the wound started!) "Deal?" "Deal."

How very wise you are, solving the problem like this by going for a partnership solution instead of trying to "win" or teach your partner how to behave. Those two tactics will just aggravate the situation.

Now let's say the conflict over the décor is not based in longtime psychological wounds. He might just really hate the blandness of your beige sheers. An all-tan house might just be too boring. This is your first home together and maybe he envisioned more color. It could be as simple as that. "What do you prefer?" is the direct, respectful question that you're going to want to be asked when you're on the other side of this conflict. That's when you'll hear, "Just not beige. How about a blue or a green in this room?" When you listen, instead of bracing yourself for a fight (after all, you have longtime issues, too!), you may find yourselves codesigning a far more beautiful, colorful room than you ever envisioned.

You don't want to be *that spouse* who makes all the decorating decisions while your spouse just defers to your every whim, right?

If you can't agree on a choice—or even when to work on the décor, which could be your issue—put off the decision until you're both ready to go. Newlyweds face a big lesson in patience when they wait for a spouse to be in a mindset to work on something they want to do *now*.

It's often a cause of conflict, but those arguments teach you to meet in the middle. Décor might be the topic, but it's really about patience and working together. Lesson learned.

When it comes to choosing new décor and furniture, the conflict now includes the *money*. Can you afford to drop $3,000 on a new couch or plasma television? One partner's dreamy plans for the home may have to hit the brakes and wait for a more affluent time in the future. Together, you'll learn the joys of delayed gratification. Many couples don't get the furniture they want until five years after their wedding. We're a rush-rush society. We want everything now. Together, as husband and wife, you'll get to make smart money decisions and put off that couch purchase for better times.

Our pet wishes are:

_____

_____

_____

The First Conflict About Pets

You want a purebred cocker spaniel, and he wants to be pet-free for a while. Again, one partner's "no" should stand as the rule. Adopting a pet is a huge commitment in time and money (veterinarian bills are expensive!). So now is when you may have to be let down gently, agree to a plan to wait for a while, or accept that you'll never have a home filled with six dogs and two cats. It doesn't matter what the issue is—money, time, allergies, worries about damage to your furniture, the fact that you travel a lot and would have to board a pet often. The key here is that one of you will want the new addition to the family, while the other has a different plan. Compromise and waiting for a better time in your life may be part of the equation for you.

When you battle about wanting a pet, it's a serious consideration about your true abilities to care for one and give it the best life possible. So if you're hearing "no" from your partner, it's not all about you and how you never get what you want. This is about a living being who deserves to be in a home where both "parents" are equally enthusiastic about its care.

CHAPTER 10

Handling Housework and Home Maintenance

Taking out the trash is a man's work. Oh, really? The division of housework between newlyweds is a very pervasive challenge, even if you've lived together for years and have established a system that works just fine for you. He cooks dinner, you do the dishes. He walks the dog. You both do your own laundry. The system that evolved naturally while you've been living together isn't going to change, right? That's not always the case. A strange thing happens when those wedding rings land on your fingers. All of a sudden, in some deep recesses of his mind or yours, there might be an expectation that a husband does the heavy lifting and all the house repairs, and the wife changes the sheets and does the grocery shopping. Slowly and quietly, these shifts may start to move into your marriage.

The First Conflict Over Who Does Which Housework

Why am I doing all the grocery shopping now?
Why am I cleaning up after the dog all the time?
Why is the clogged toilet my responsibility? You can use a plunger, too.

No one knows why expectations slide into old-fashioned roles, and I'm sure teams of psychologists could have a party with the inner sanctums of our minds, but let's not get too analytical here. The fact is that many newlyweds find themselves facing what starts off as an unspoken expectation of what each partner will now do for the household now that they both wear the new hats of husband and wife. And if you don't say something about any unfairness of housework expectations, it's going to simmer and boil over.

As with most newlywed lessons, the first few months are going to be a learning experience—especially if you didn't live together before marriage and you each have "your way" of doing things. So I suggest a Housework Summit, where you'll both sit down to decide who is going to handle which aspects of the home maintenance and cleaning. (See page 47 for your chart on household chores). And this can be more fun than you expect! When you spell out the needs and demands of your space—such as walking the dog or cleaning the fireplace—you can choose to see this list as more of an "Aren't We Lucky" inventory. *It's a blessing to have a home to care for!* So start off with that statement.

Next, talk about which tasks you love to do, never minding the "traditional" roles. Husbands may be the cooks in the family, so they'll be only too happy to take on dinners and breakfasts. You might decide as a couple that you'd both like to do your own laundry. (You don't like the scented fabric softener, and he does.) So you're going to split that job. As for lawn care, you'd like to take the wheel of the riding mower.

Facing each task with a conversation lifts you above the silence and the stewing that often comes with trying to avoid the topic. You agree to share some jobs, divide some, and take turns with others. And you absolutely *can* talk about your history with certain tasks, such as, "It always bothered me that my father would come home from work, throw his briefcase down on the table, and demand, 'What's for dinner?' I hated seeing my mother drop everything and run to whip up a dinner to please him. And then he never said thank you." This simple story tells your spouse what he shouldn't do. A brilliant way to beat this challenge is to say, "I'd really appreciate it if we could food shop together on Sunday so that we can both choose the meals for the week," or "I'd really appreciate it if you would greet me when you come home, ask how my day is, and then we can both decide what's for dinner and who's cooking." You've just been honest and open, and your spouse—who's not a mind-reader—will appreciate your pointing out that great big land mine in your inner world. He'd rather know what to watch out for than step on it with an innocent, "Hey, hon, what's for dinner?" that makes you burst into tears.

One big challenge is when you take on a chore and he doesn't think you do it well enough. *That's* a big trap for newlyweds, so be on the lookout for the perfection factor in either of you. Instead of taking it personally, chalk it up to "Okay, let's switch this one task for now."

Never, ever sink into the position of allowing your partner to micromanage your dusting, vacuuming, dishwashing, or other tasks. If you agree to adjust your ways to your partner's, you may feel like you are slowly disappearing, and that's when resentment sets in. Make an agreement now that you'll both have to adjust to how the other does the job. The bed linens might not be ironed. Get over it. You might not feel the need to keep the sink clear of all spoons, since it's not urgent to you to get everything in the dishwasher *now*. It may sound laughable, but this is what newlyweds fight over. *Why can't you do it my way?*

So prepare yourselves for a few months of adjusting and accepting how each of you will handle the housework. You can always have a new Housework Summit to make a few changes later. When the two of you show each other that you're invested in creating a home that gives you equal say and equal power in its maintenance, it will be a happier home.

It may take a few tries to organize your system.

The First Conflict Over Paying for Experts to Come Fix Things

This is one of the most surprising conflicts that can arise for newlyweds. The very act of calling an electrician might be taken as a message that "you don't think I can do this" by your spouse. Ridiculous, right? Most early newlywed fights are ridiculous, filled with things taken too personally and blown out of proportion. Calling an expert to fix a leaky faucet or flickering light isn't a message that your spouse is inept, but maybe he has invested a lot of thought into the problem, and your calling a pro means you don't think he is one. Avoid this unexpected newlywed scuffle by talking over any plans to consult with experts before you make the call. It's not about getting permission. It's just an agreement to be 100% partners.

The other part of this conflict might be sticker shock. A plumber can charge you a few hundred dollars just to come out and *look* at the problem you have with your toilet. Many newlyweds admit they're on a learning curve, especially if they didn't own a home before marriage and are ripe for trial and error when it comes to issues like this one. You might be partnering on very expensive firsts for your home, and navigating the crowded field of professionals and tradespeople out there is a scary thing. Every newlywed couple runs into a few unprofessional pros, those who don't do the job well but do a fine job of billing and accepting a check. So as newlyweds, this may be your first time getting suckered by a shady electrician or drywall contractor. This can hurt very much. You're a brilliant career person, you're educated, you have street smarts. But that little old man who came in to do your drywall absolutely fleeced you.

It's important to have your spouse's back when these things happen. Don't shame him or her for being taken by a con artist. And definitely, never bring this unfortunate situation up again, such as in future fights when some house project doesn't go as planned. Your spouse is *not* the one who always hires the bad professional. It would be quite cruel of you to even joke about a prior bad experience. Your gift to your spouse is shrugging away the inevitable bad event and chalking it up to a learning experience. You're both learning as you go. What's important is that you're safe from the other's scorn and judgment.

WARNING BELLS!

Your partner's mistake in hiring the wrong plumber *isn't* great cocktail party story material. So don't share a "my wife is so dumb that . . ." tale with your friends or colleagues, even if less-evolved buddies are enjoying humiliating their wives with such stories. Would you want your spouse to share stories of the embarrassing things you've done in the past? Humiliation is a death knell to a marriage, so tell a good joke instead.

The First Conflict Over Now vs. Later

This is one of those sneaky issues that starts off as a little annoyance that your spouse tends to procrastinate on finishing projects, returning calls, paying bills, or any number of other tasks associated with your home life. And then it grows and grows into a big, big conflict. Especially if you're a "get it done early" type who can't relax unless everything is in order. A stack of bills lying on the dining room table can lead to a ton of anxiety, even if there's still a few days until the due dates.

The underlying issues, getting magnified each day, are "you don't care about what I need" or "other things are more important to you than being on time with our bills" (even if there are still days left to pay!), and the ultradangerous statement of "you're just delaying because you know it bothers me." These are just illustrations of the kinds of emotional, or overly emotional, interpretations that can arise when one of you is early and one of you is more laid-back.

I'm not going to say that you need to change and be more laid-back if you're the one who needs order. That's a part of your personality, and it's not going to change at the flick of a switch. Nor is your partner's style of paying at the last minute online or over the phone. This conflict is a good one to have, since it allows you to get your frustrations out, then have some make-up sex before you work together on a better plan, a compromise on now vs. later. You both have valid reasons why your timing seems preferable, and you do want to respect your partner's needs. So talk it out, and perhaps agree to pay all bills a week before they're due to give you that peace of mind you need. If it's mail that needs to be opened, agree to a Sunday night mail sorting session in front of the TV. If it's a home project that's languishing, set a date to get whichever tool you need, block that day off the calendar, tell his mother that you have an important date that day, so no he can't go running to help her pick out geraniums (or whatever attention-grabbing request she's thrown to delay your own plans—more on in-law issues in a coming chapter!), and just get it done.

Direct communication is always best. Let your partner know that too many open projects stress you out, just like too many open applications slow down a computer. "How about we take one day this weekend and blast through all of these half-done things?" could be the perfect solution to clear the slate, so that you can put your new now vs. later plan into action fully and with dedication.

The First Conflict Over Organizational Plans

Your spouse has said it before: "I'm a little bit anal about organization" or "I'm so unorganized" on the flip side. If you have different styles when it comes to organization in your home, you're going to clash. Maybe you don't want the spices alphabetized. Maybe your spouse doesn't want your DVDs sorted by genre. Maybe you don't want to color coordinate your towels in the linen closet. Maybe your spouse can't stand having so many boxes in the garage.

GET A GREAT GUIDE

You don't need to hire a professional organizer, unless you have a mountain of belongings and are feeling just too stuck to make any headway. Check out great organization supply sites like www.spacesavers.com, www.target.com, www.containerstore.com, and www.bedbathandbeyond.com for storage solutions that will be *fun* for the two of you to work with as you devise your own home organization plan.

Again, you have to compromise and find a plan that works, because you'll feel controlled if your ultraorganized spouse has turned your home into a labeled, plastic-bin-filled laboratory. You won't live in peace if you're afraid to move anything out of place. Organization is one thing, control is another. And that's exactly what the far extreme is, when one spouse starts moving the other spouse's stuff into an arrangement that *they* want. Yes, those home organizing shows make it look like so much fun, and how awesome is it to get an extra ten feet of clear space in the garage? But at what cost?

Neither of you can justify taking over the organization of your home.

So choose smaller categories, such as getting one bin for all of your wrapping paper supplies. Getting organized does feel great, when you do it the right way, when you work on it together. But a "no" has to remain a "no." "No, I don't want all of my nail polishes arranged from lights to darks in the medicine cabinet. No, I don't want my underwear moved into a different drawer because that will match how you have yours organized."

Organization is supposed to make life easier, not slow down your daily activities when you have to keep running down to the basement to get the cooking pans you need. Agree to try out new organizing plans, but if high-up storage is not working for the shorter member of your household, something needs to shift.

Yelling out "It's my house, too!" isn't going to solve anything if said in anger. The only way to create an organized home plan is to take it piece by piece, make no moves without consulting the other, and be honest if the first organization plan is a bust. Don't do too much at once, especially when you're first married. You might be comfortable with change, but it'll only freak out your partner who is already adjusting to so many changes of married life. Baby steps.

CHAPTER 11

Everyday Life

From sex to time spent apart to intimate conversations, the balance of a great marriage depends on careful footwork during everyday life. It's often the little things that cause conflict between newlyweds. Adjusting to married life can be tough if you've created a fantasy of endless romantic dinners and walks on the beach, because everyday life is full of responsibilities and too long to-do lists. So read this chapter with a mindset of "I have to remember *not* to do this." It also offers a way to understand when your spouse boils over out of nowhere. Little pressures add up.

The First Conflict About Your Sex Life

Your friends may have joked that sex stops after the wedding. Life gets busy, and you will not be *getting* busy—at least not to the degree that you did before the wedding, perhaps before the engagement. If you were filled with wedding stress, your sex life may have declined, so you may be looking forward to newlywed bliss filled with endless, romantic fantasies of dreamy seductions. You believed married sex would be *hot*. Or you may have listened to your friends and resigned yourself to a life of barely there intimacy.

Whatever your beliefs and expectations, that first clash over who wants more and who always has a headache can rock you to the core. How can your partner be so dismissive of you? He comes home from work, and you're decked out in your best lingerie and heels, working for an hour on your hair and makeup, and he says he's too tired, and that he needs "decompression time" when he gets home, and why can't you ever get that straight? Such a rejection feels awful. Especially when you change out of your sexy outfit and get into sweats.

The first thing you need to establish is a kinder, gentler rule about saying now's not the time. Being married doesn't give either of you license to reject the other insensitively. And it doesn't mean you have to perform when you're not up to it. So tell your spouse you need to set up some ground rules for the "not now, honey" moments. Maybe you do have to grasp that he needs decompression time right when he gets home, and not dress up to surprise him. Maybe suggest sex in the morning, rather than at night after he's been studying or doing work around the house.

Spontaneity is terrific, but sometimes you can't just jump on your spouse. And sometimes, you need to jump on your spouse more.

Ask him what his downtimes are, and respect them. Tell him what your downtimes are. Give him a little bit of notice, such as letting him know that tonight would be a great night for some "alone time" (wink, wink). And learn to *not* take it personally if your spouse is too tired or distracted with work issues to really connect with you. It's very important that you remove any message of hurt that you display to make your spouse feel guilty (and that's not an easy thing to admit you're doing.) And you absolutely cannot use any words of cruelty either way, with those dreaded "you always" and "you never" statements. What you're after here is a better plan to make sure both of your needs are being met.

If lovemaking is out of the question tonight, how about a make-out session? That alone could give you the sense of connection you crave. Your spouse who just doesn't have the steam to perform might agree that intimacy is what's needed here, and that cuddling could be a great way to give you both what you need.

DON'T READ "IS HE CHEATING?" ARTICLES

Just because it's been a few weeks doesn't mean he has a woman on the side. Those scare-tactic articles you see in so many magazines use fear to drive consumerism. "Buy these clothes and keep his interest!" "Look younger with this face cream and he'll stay faithful." It's a funny thing about many of these articles: They're just like health articles that give you a list of common symptoms, such as fatigue and irritability, and then tell you that you have a dozen different ailments. Steer clear of the paranoia-publishing track and focus on the truth and reality of your partnership instead. Don't overdramatize this sexual slump or you could drive your spouse away. If you're calm and supportive and patient, intimacy will return to you.

Now if your partner's sex drive is way, way different than it used to be, you need to discuss why that is. He might be depressed. There might be symptoms of stress and anxiety that make him want to pull back. These are issues that, if they're truly disrupting your marriage, you need to encourage your mate to seek help for. Short-term counseling and even medication might be what's needed here. A loving spouse thinks of his or her partner's wellness before any sense of ego. Be ready to direct your partner to a good health-care provider to get a checkup. Low energy could be anemia. A simple blood test can report what's going on inside of your partner. And health issues often affect sex drive. If it's you who's never in the mood, the same rule applies. It's an investment in your marriage to seek help, so that your arguments over differing sexual appetites don't tear your marriage to pieces.

The First Conflict About Private Time vs. Together Time

This is a bad one, because one of you may have to admit that you're being too clingy. Everyone needs time alone. You have to maintain your own friendships and social life so that your partner doesn't get smothered by a belief that he's your whole world. And vice versa.

When the pressure builds, an attack can come out of nowhere. One of you didn't say something soon enough about wanting more alone time, and now the resentment has built up to the point where you just snap and say something very, very mean. Amazing how comfortable we are yelling at our partner when we would never say the same things to strangers or acquaintances. "Get a life!" is not something that you should ever say to your partner, nor should you ever hear it from the person who vowed to love you in good times and in bad.

While it's true that a request for more alone time should be voiced to a trusting partner, some spouses say they don't want to hurt their partner's feelings, especially in the first few months of marriage when you

"Every human being needs his or her own identity—we panic when we lose our sense of self in too much togetherness. This is often a root cause of fighting—couples fight when they can't find a way to get space. Each of you should have some separate friends and interests. It gives you something to talk about after you reconnect."

—Tina Tessina, Ph.D., Author of *Money, Sex, and Kids*

want to just *be* together all the time. It may be hard for your spouse to say, "back off," because you're always cooing about how nice it is to spend another Friday night at home watching movies. He might be losing his mind because he misses his friends and wants time with them.

The key word here is *missing*. Listen up, because here's one of the golden keys to a better first year of marriage: You both have to work in separate time so that you can *miss* each other. Missing each other leads to appreciation, and it only happens when you create a good amount of distance between you on a regular basis. So if this blowout leads to rage and insults, you'll both have to apologize and be gentle in explaining that you love your partner, but your soul needs some time by yourself or with other friends or relatives. It's no reflection on your partner or how in love you are. It's just a human thing. Everyone needs solitude and the freedom to keep their identities intact.

Experts say that being too crowded elicits a fight-or-flight mechanism that's deeply ingrained in our wiring, so those arguments, insults, and attacks are sometimes subconscious. It's the animal in you fighting for survival and security. This is very true. After the blowup, you're out of breath and in disbelief that you reacted so strongly.

WARNING!

If you're angry or pouty about your spouse wanting to go out with friends instead of spending time with you, you may have an insecurity issue to address. Would he have kept dating you in the beginning if you were always demanding 100% of his time? Would you have dated him if he never wanted you to go out with your friends? It's no different now. It may be that you have moved recently and you don't have any close friends nearby with whom you can go out for a drink or see a movie. Your spouse might be the only person you know well, besides your colleagues and neighbors who are just acquaintances right now. You haven't had enough time to make new friends, so your spouse is practically your entire social outlet.

This is a *very* important problem to address right now—and enlist your spouse's help! No, it's not pathetic to admit, "I don't have close friends around here yet." You're telling your spouse you recognize that you both need social circles. You're working to expand your friendship horizons. That's great news to a spouse who feels smothered, so he or she might help you connect with colleagues or their spouses with whom you have shared interests, or walk with you over to meet the neighbors. You might also decide to volunteer, either solo or as a couple, through www.volunteermatch.org. It takes effort to make new friends as an adult, but you'll find that people *want* to connect and spend social time together. It may be easier than you think, and "getting a life" will help prevent conflicts with your spouse.

If you're both aware that it's a human need to have time apart, using this argument as a learning experience, you'll wisely build more private time and nights out with friends into the routine of your life together. People fall in love in the spaces in between seeing each other during those first few dating months, that time when you can't wait for your beloved to arrive in three days—and people stay in love when you make yourself a little bit more scarce. It may seem counterintuitive, but it's a universal code of advice that relationship therapists share with their clients.

The First Conflict About Friends

This is an offshoot of the previous topic, where conflict arises, not from the fact that one of you wants to take a night off to spend time with friends, but rather *who* these friends are. We all worry about negative influences on our spouse and our married lives, and sometimes your partner's friends can be a challenge. You might not like his rowdy college buddies with their frat-boy mentalities and sketchy pasts. He might not like your high-drama friends with their midnight phone calls to cry about their boyfriends. Sometimes, your spouse's friends can add a bad element of surprise to your life when your spouse calls you for a ride home after they've been drinking for hours. "It's just another night out with the boys." And you don't like how your spouse seems to lose a bunch of IQ points when he's with them. Or he might not like how you act when you're out with your friends.

The bottom line is: Like them or not, they're your spouse's friends. And unless they're always getting *arrested*, you're better off just accepting them, shaking off their character flaws and annoying qualities, and just being true to your partner, because the kind of life your spouse shared with them is likely to fade organically. You can't end your spouse's pre-you socializing patterns.

GUYS' TIP

When it's your wife who disapproves of your friends, that can put you in a tough position. These people are important to you, and you just don't see why she hates your buddies so much. Okay, so maybe she's heard about drunken, wild nights and she doesn't appreciate the way they talk about the women in their lives. But why does she give *you* a hassle about it?

She doesn't want them to influence your decisions. You could assure her all day and all night that your friends wouldn't corrupt you, but it's still a raw nerve for her. Maybe she had an ex whose friends did corrupt him. We all have personal histories and wounds, and your friends are certainly aggravating hers. So make an agreement with her . . . if you don't like some of her friends either, neither of you will guilt-trip the other about making plans with friends. Neither of you will make the other "pay" for spending time with buddies with interrogations or silent treatments, and neither of you will criticize the other's friends. You'll both just accept that you don't think highly of certain friends, but you trust your spouse always to do the right thing while in their company. Your wife wants to hear you say, "My friends could never corrupt me or change how I feel about you." She'd say the same to you. But just like family, your circles of friends are part of the package. It's something everyone has to learn to accept, and that applies to your dislike of her annoying friends, too.

So shrink this issue down to size. Don't fight with your spouse about your disapproval of his friends unless you have to go bail him out of jail. It's one thing to wisely want to steer him away from truly dangerous friends, but if you look at this honestly, you'll see that his friends aren't a threat to your marriage—how you treat your spouse *about* these friends is the real threat. And again, the same applies to your partner.

Now let's say that a friend drives drunk or has a drug problem. It's perfectly understandable for you to express to your spouse that you don't want him hurt in an accident or arrested for being in a car with illegal substances. He could wreck his life. That should be expressed in a calm, planned discussion, not when he stumbles in drunk at 2 A.M. and you're in full anger mode because he didn't call. He's not going to hear a word you say, and that's a big fight waiting to happen. Timing is everything, so save the talk for later.

A great investment in your marriage is finding a way to appreciate your spouse's friends, being nice to them when they visit, finding things to talk about, socializing together when the occasion arises, and embracing the part of your spouse's world that preceded you. You don't have to love these friends, but it's best for you if you can live with their presence in your life—and maybe even find things that you do like about them. Your spouse will love it if he or she finds they're growing on you. No one wants to feel guilty for hanging out with their friends. You'd just become the nag for disapproving and guilt-tripping, or suggesting that your friends would be better for you to spend all your free time with. That's a disaster for your marriage.

The First Conflict About Sleeping Schedules and Needs

Everyone needs to sleep, and everyone has their own sleeping routines, such as sleeping in until noon on the weekends. If you're newly living together, you might run into a conflict about differing sleep schedules.

You might see the weekend as a time to get things done, run errands, go out for breakfast . . . but you don't exactly want to jump out of bed without waking your partner.

Somewhere in your mind, you think it's wonderful to snuggle in against your spouse or initiate morning sex. But your partner turns away from you, grumbling.

This is a little-known conflict among newlyweds, because it's not covered heavily in the media the way newlywed money fights and waning sex lives are made into headlines. But encroaching on your partner's shut-eye is one of those lifestyle issues that can drive a wedge between the newly married.

Do you feel comfortable going to bed while your partner stays up to watch television? Do you feel comfortable doing your own thing in the morning while your spouse sleeps for a few more hours? These are signs that you have a healthy amount of personal distance between you,

NO JUMPING ON THE BED!

Remember: Little kids often burst into their sleeping parents' rooms and jump on the bed, wanting their attention, being loud. You do *not* want your partner to see you as a needy child. It's poison to a marriage when one partner becomes the kid, expecting the partner to "parent" his or her needs with attention at any time of day. That's not a marriage of equals. No one wants that pressure. If your spouse feels responsible for your happiness at the expense of his or her own needs, you become a big burden. And your marriage will be in big trouble.

that you can fill a few hours without needing to be by your partner's side, and that you can respect one of your partner's most basic needs. Take a moment now to think about that. Perhaps you can go out for a walk or a run while your partner snoozes. Perhaps you can go to another room and catch up on your reading as a new morning routine of your own, with the house quiet and peaceful.

And if you're the sleeper, and your partner's the early riser, you need to be the one to tackle this conversation before it turns into a disaster. "Honey, I really need to get at least nine hours of sleep on the weekends in order to feel good. As much as I love waking up with you, I don't want it to get to the point where I'm annoyed with you for waking me up early." You're being kind and gentle, not going into how angry you *currently* are. You're giving your partner a chance to work together to prevent a problem. It's a fair and loving style of communication, especially important in matters of intimacy. You can't convey healthy requests from a place of anger. It just doesn't work.

You may have to remind your partner a few times, or you might need a few reminders yourself. It often takes a few tries to unlearn a habit, but once you grasp this issue and respect your partner's need for sleep in the morning, you'll find ways to turn your own morning into a positive time for yourself with that run or that pleasure reading. You're self-sufficient, and you can love your partner just as much from the next room . . . more so even, when you're not being needy.

The First Conflict About Weekend Plan Expectations

Building a life together means honoring equally what each of you would like, and when it comes down to the weekend, you might clash over differing expectations on how you'll spend that time. One of you wants to run errands or work on house remodeling or design projects, and the other wants to spend half the morning on the couch watching *The*

Soup and *E! News*. One of you needs downtime, and the other is anxious about wasting time. Or, one of you has a rich family life with lots of relatives' birthday parties and traditional Sunday night dinners with your parents and siblings, and the other doesn't want every weekend with *your* group.

This conflict can be another golden opportunity to create some healthy ground rules for your weekend once the dust settles on your first fight over weekend plans. Now don't be scared by the term "ground rules." This isn't a parent-child thing, but rather an equal-partners thing, and a wise way of communicating to prevent future battles. (Ever notice how you fight over the same things again and again because no one puts a solution on the table?). Your ground-rules conversation for this conflict can include the following:

❖ "I love how close you are with your family, and I love all of them very much, too. They're wonderful people. I'm just not excited about spending *every* Sunday night with them. I know you can sense when I'm anxious to get out of there, so how about we set a new plan? How about I go every other week, you go every week, and on nights when I'm not there, you stay as late as you want?" That's the perfect compromise.

❖ "When you make weekend plans without checking with me, I feel like you're running our social life. I don't want this to turn into a problem, so I'd love it if you'd give me a call or shoot me an e-mail about it before you commit us to a plan. Thanks."

❖ "How about we take one weekend a month when each of us will spend time with our friends or families? I love being with you as much as possible, but I'm starting to miss my friends. I don't want to drift from them, and I'm sure you don't want to drift from your friends, either."

❖ "I know the errands need to get done each weekend, and I don't want you to feel like they're all on you. So how about we make an adjustment to our errand schedule and go grocery shopping

THE B-WORD

"Boundaries" is the key word here. You may be married, but you're individuals with different needs. To be a good partner, you need to make your own boundaries clear. If you need to skip a family party, just say so. "I love your family, but I really need a quiet afternoon on my own." To which the other partner should reply, "Okay. No problem," not "What are my parents going to think if you don't show up?! I always go to *your* family's parties! Why can't you come to mine?!" Don't be that spouse. Give your partner some time alone, and enjoy those weekly family parties as a confident solo act. The best marriages are between those who can spend a few hours apart, because coming home to a spouse who misses you is pure bliss.

on Monday night when *American Idol* isn't on, instead of spending every Saturday morning buying food? I just like my Saturday mornings to be open."

✢ "If we have a plan and I need to back out of it, please don't take it personally. It's not any reflection of how much time I want to spend with you. It's that I'm feeling overwhelmed at work and exhausted from this wedding debt, so I need a little bit of time to relax more, or work out, instead of socializing with friends right now."

Your First Fight Over Nothing

Sometimes you're going to fight over *nothing*. You've had a ton of work stress, the wedding bills have you mired in debt, your sister is being whiny and needy, and you're bloated and your jeans don't fit. Then your husband walks into the room and asks if you used his shaving cream and you explode on him. Or he comes home from a long day at work, his jeans don't fit after the honeymoon, and he snaps at you because you want to watch *What Not to Wear* again tonight. In our busy, hectic, stressed-out lives, it can take one small thing to cause a senseless explosion. And then it's an argument.

The first time this happens, it can stun you both. Where did that attack come from?

You might be used to these miniblowups throughout your relationship together, but the first one as a married couple can come with a few added elements. Your husband might attempt to diagnose you with "Oh, you're just upset about the wedding bills," which may be true, but it's the last thing he should have said to you.

Here's the key to the first fight over nothing: Be ready for it ahead of time. In calmer moments, create a code for it. Just say, "I just read in this book that newlyweds have to prepare for fights over nothing when stress builds up, so the next time that happens with us, how about we say 'I'm having a boiling-over moment'?" You pinpoint the problem, which is that you're on overload. And then your partner knows that you just need to vent, nothing should be taken personally, and there's a hug and a foot rub waiting right after the explosion.

This pretalk will arm you with a collection of soothers, which you can request from each other. Here are some ideas:

+ "The next time I snap at you over nothing, don't blame PMS. What I really want is for you to hug me and kiss my neck and say you love me."

* "The next time I snap at you over nothing, it's not going to work if you tell me how to solve the problem. I just want you to let me vent, nod, and hold my hand."

+ "If I'm feeling like I'm going to explode, I'm going to say I'm having a pressure-cooker moment, so please just give me some time to myself."

Asking for time to yourself is a great request newlyweds can make of each other, and it's a gift you give each other by not adding fuel to the fire by taking it personally and whining that your partner doesn't want you to help. You can't help. It's just a mood, and moods pass when the moody one gets what he or she needs to siphon off the pressure. As you know, it can be more annoying when your partner tries to comfort you. So make an agreement now that if privacy is needed, you'll honor that boundary.

When you establish this practice now, you'll have fewer fights later. It's the couples who don't voice their needs for this common conflict who keep repeating the same mistakes, hurting each other more and more even if they don't intend to.

Your First Fight Over "Newlywed 19" Weight Gain

So many brides and grooms gain weight on their honeymoon. With all the delectable gourmet meals at the resort, snack foods by the pool, calorie-filled frozen drinks, and a hedonistic getaway of lying by the ocean with no cares in the world, you're coming home at least five pounds heavier. Some people come back ten pounds heavier if they really indulged.

Now, add weight gain from all of the dinners with family, late-night pizza orders, being too tired to cook healthier meals, being too entranced with being newlyweds to get to the gym, money stress, and adjustment stress—and you may have packed on a few more pounds.

The danger comes when you or your spouse sense disapproval from the other over how you look. Your weight gain shows, and you have less energy because of it. And deep down, you feel really awful about it. So that's when you might be overly sensitive and overreact to the simple moment when your spouse puts his hand on your stomach while you're laying on the couch and gives it a little squeeze. He didn't mean it as an insult. But that's how you took it. So you're off to the races with "You think I'm fat!" or "Don't squeeze it, you jerk!" Maybe you're not overreacting. Maybe your partner feels he or she is helping you by saying, "Hey, nice muffin top." Your spouse is probably not a complete jerk . . . maybe this teasing is how his parents motivated him to be more active in his youth. He never took offense at his family's jabs, so why would you?

Yes, most of us say "No, you look great" when our partner asks if they look fat in those jeans, but we know they're really asking because they *feel* fat in those jeans. Pretty soon, they're eating a healthier break-fast, cutting out cola, and doing sit-ups during the evening news. You didn't need to say anything. They got to a point of frustration with how they look and feel, and they're doing something about it. Bravo!

But the real world doesn't always work like that.

Sometimes your spouse makes a comment about your muffin top, and you feel like you've been stabbed in the heart by the person you trust most in this world. "Well, I'm *sorry* I don't have *time* to work out, while I'm doing *your* laundry and cleaning the house on my *own* with any spare time I have!" is the classic victim response. You want to hurt your spouse right back. It's an animal instinct—one you need to control.

However this ugly conflict arises, or if it comes in the form of a health concern, such as a high-glucose test at a checkup, or a knee that's hurting, the important thing is that the conflict should lead to a discussion about loving your partner, wanting to help protect their health so that you can live a long and happy life together and not put yourselves at risk for any diseases. Better to work on it now when it's just nineteen pounds of newlywed weight gain rather than thirty or forty.

How do you deal with the emotional injury of an insensitive comment about your weight? It's always how your partner makes you *feel* that's more important than what's said. And if you have existing wounds about body image, that "muffin top" comment would be more hurtful than your spouse could ever know. This is where you ask for an apology and say, "I really can't have you making fun of me, or calling me names . . . shame *isn't* a motivator for me. It just makes me trust you less. So please don't say mean things to me. I would never say something like that to you."

Of course, humor may be your way of communicating, but that opens the door for passive-aggressive sniping. "Yes, I may have a muffin top, but you have an entire bakery hanging over your belt, mister" isn't exactly funny. You're laughing, but you just smacked your spouse with an equally hurtful insult. Guys have body image issues, too.

As newlyweds, you have some conflict-resolution skills under your belt already. You've clashed over a few things, and maybe he's made an unwelcome comment about your being bloated. But this might be new to you. Newlyweds get into trouble when they feel they can be brutally honest with each other now that they're married. There's a big difference between honesty and *brutal* honesty . . . the word *brutal* is in there.

No matter what you're clashing about, you have to be sensitive to your partner's existing wounds, and not leave injuries that last. Those who don't adhere to these rules are called abusive partners. I'm not being dramatic. An abusive partner says things to shatter the victim's self-confidence to the point where the partner is fragmented and afraid of the next insult or injury. You *don't* want to be *that* person. Just put name-calling and teasing right out of your playbook because that's junior-high tactics. That's abuse thinly disguised as concern.

RUN FOR HELP

At any signs of abuse, run—do not walk—to counseling. An objective professional can spell out even unintentional abusive patterns, and both spouses will listen to an authority figure more than they would to each other. Spend the $150 on a session or two. It's far less expensive than a divorce.

So how can you better broach the subject of weight gain in your partner? Choose your moment well. You'll know it when it's upon you. Your spouse might be trying to find a suit that fits, complaining that he's gotten fat, and that could be your perfect opportunity to bring up a suggestion. "I've put a few pounds on, too, so I'd really love it if we could start working out together, maybe every other night after work. What do you think would be the most fun? Tennis? Basketball? Biking? I see neighbors walking together all the time, and that looks like so much fun." Center this initial approach on the activity you'd like to share, and don't jump into too many other categories, such as not ordering pizza anymore. You might have to scale back your usual enthusiasm, or else your partner may feel like you're running the show. Just one commitment at a time would do wonders.

You can also spell out the health benefits, such as saying "a one-pound weight loss takes six pounds of pressure off of your knees," shifting the focus from the emotionally loaded issue of how your partner looks to how teaming up for weight loss will turn into an improvement in lifestyle and well-being. A few pluses can't hurt.

What your spouse really wants to hear is that you love him or her fully, no matter if he or she is carrying a few extra pounds. We can all get self-conscious about our bodies, so be hands-on from minute one with plenty of hugs and affection, and the two of you can take the next step into action with a fitness plan, some healthier foods that just happen to show up in your shopping cart, and suggestions for activity-oriented dates, such as going biking instead of going to the movies. You become "the fun spouse" again, busting you out of your rut, and joining your spouse in healthier endeavors.

You do need to allow your spouse to adjust to his or her own new fitness and health plan. You can't sign your partner up for boot camp and expect total compliance. No one likes to be dragged into a responsibility like this. So be that cool partner who has an independent life as well, and choose some new fitness classes or DVDs for yourself, leaving your spouse to choose a field of fitness of his own. You don't have to do everything together, but you do need to notice and say something when some of that "Newlywed 19" starts to melt away. "Your arms look great" and "I can see it in your face. You've lost a few pounds. Congratulations!" are the hallmarks of supportive spouses.

And what's a hallmark of spouses who get fit together? Let's just say they spend a lot less time with clothes on.

CHAPTER 12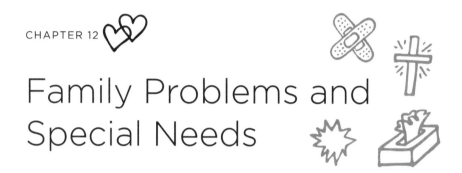

Family Problems and Special Needs

Every family has tough times: illnesses, divorce, financial problems. And as members of two extended families, you're deeply connected to the traumas and trials that both of your families face. And you may have some tough times of your own. In the best of families, everyone circles the wagons and comes to the aid of those in need. When difficulties are long-lasting, the pressure of being scared and drained can weigh on your relationship. Remember to care for yourself, replenish your energy, and feed your marriage during these times so that you can remain a helpful member of the team.

The First Time Your Families Need Special Care

When a parent, sibling, or grandparent falls ill or needs special care, the entire family usually comes together to help in any way they can. As newlyweds, you absolutely cannot expect that you're exempt from caretaking. This is where "in sickness and in health" come into play, and it *is* valid when it's an important family member's health in question. So put away any expectations of being the center of your spouse's attention during this time. If it's your parent in the hospital, release yourself from the pressures of being a perfect new wife, because this emotionally charged time is going to sap you of some of your energy and strength. A good spouse knows that he or she is loved even without the outward signs of affection or attention when the family is going through a tough time. No one would ever forgive you for being whiny and demanding to go on your usual Friday night date if a loved one is in the hospital.

As a new member of the family, this is your time to show your dedication to your spouse and his loved ones by pitching in—watching his sister's kids while she takes a break from daily caretaking, cooking for the sick family member or for the caretaking family, cleaning your brother-in-law's kitchen while he shuttles his father to chemo treatments, or taking a shift at the hospital so everyone else can take a night off. These are your relatives now, so the tough time is yours as well . . . and you can bring some light to it by helping out. Even the smallest act of help, a hug, a phone call to say "what can I do?" is a loving gesture of familial closeness and caring.

If the caretaking time is extended, a loving newlywed takes on more of the responsibilities in the home so that the spouse can go help his family. This is not the time to gauge how much your spouse loves you, because you will never rank above an ill family member. Don't even try that juvenile test. Your 100% support is all that's acceptable now. Life will get back to its usual routine in time. For now, your support is needed.

The First Loss or Tragedy in the Family

No matter which of you has lost a loved one, the other needs to be a comforting, supportive partner no matter where the other is in the grieving process. A common newlywed mistake is to want your partner to come out of their grief, to stop suffering, as soon as possible. But the loving intention can come off as insensitivity. They're not going to get over it any more quickly because you baked a pie or because it's been six months. Marriages can crumble when one partner is not unconditionally supportive of the other, so during this heart-wrenching time, your job is to give solace, to listen, to hug, and to hold, and not to take outbursts personally. In times of great pain and fear, we may say things we don't mean, and sometimes a grieving person can lash out at those who try to comfort them. Just let it go. Ask what your partner needs and give it to them. Even if it's time alone and silence that's being requested, he's not shutting you out. He's protecting himself. Or, you're protecting yourself with your own request for alone time.

Grief hits everyone differently, and everyone needs to find their own way through the dark time. As a supportive newlywed, you have to allow that process to evolve, and find a gentle way to suggest grief counseling if your partner is experiencing deep depression or exhibiting destructive behavior. Offer to go with him. Remind him that there's no shame in asking for help. That no one has to bear pain alone. You are there for each other, no matter what each of you may need.

This may be a long season of mourning. So consider the grieving person's needs as paramount, and meet your own needs as well.

The First Time You're Sick and Need TLC

You've probably supported your partner through a bout of the flu or a sinus infection before, visiting with chicken soup, picking up ginger ale and crackers, driving him to the doctor. These loving acts are the essence of a married partnership, where you'd do anything to help each other feel better.

The first time either of you gets sick during the first year of marriage, these same loving and caretaking steps need to be practiced. And newlyweds who are living together for the first time need to be aware that they may have to take on the spouse's household duties for the week. You'd be surprised how many newlyweds forget this! They get so used to the other spouse doing the grocery shopping that it doesn't even occur to them that the chore won't get done this week. And then the sick partner gets angry. "You're taking me for granted!" is the common cry from the weary and weakened partner. So take this as a warning that you have to step it up one more notch and take care of all the household duties while your spouse recovers. And get him or her a special recovery present while you're out running errands. We all love to get little surprises, and a new DVD or some comfy socks makes your partner feel well-loved and nurtured.

When it's something more serious than the sniffles, such as a cancer scare, when initial test results come back with something strange and further tests are needed, newlyweds can get shaken to their core. You just got married! How can something so scary happen right now? No one has guaranteed protection from tragedies, so if you or your spouse experience a scary medical situation or a dangerous diagnosis that's going to change your lives in the coming months, the number one thing you need to do is discuss as a couple the steps you will take together from this point on. Your spouse might request that you respect his privacy and not tell your entire family about his news just yet, and you have to honor that. Now is not the time for betrayal. This is a very serious time, a very traumatic era in your new marriage, and any misstep now will have lasting repercussions. You are a team, working together to make the best decisions about a health issue. So you'll avoid those who overreact, you'll listen only to your medical team, and you'll do everything you can to stay positive and supportive for your spouse or for yourself. If you need to vent, vent to a trusted friend. Keep your fears under control, and give yourselves the best chance of beating whatever challenge is ahead of you.

See pages 237–238 for more on caregiving during medical crises.

The First Time a Family Battle Affects Your Relationship

Who doesn't have some lunacy in their family? Siblings battle over who owes the other money, parents play favorites, everyone's fighting over grandma's jewelry . . . These kinds of family battles leach into your relationship when they affect *you.* Your partner doesn't want to see you upset, so he may say that your sister is a greedy, selfish witch. He may form a bad opinion of your father when he calls and says something that hurts you. Here's a common one: You might get angry at your spouse for *not* getting angry at your sister or father in your defense! "Why aren't you outraged at this?!" Simple. He doesn't get outraged at what he's seen to be the family pattern: everyone argues, and then everyone's fine at Sunday dinner. Your family's battle patterns are very clear to so-called outsiders. You're just a group that clashes, your hierarchy is clear, and you keep having the same fights over and over. Your spouse knows you're going to forgive your sister eventually, so why would he get angry now? Is this the truth for your family circle?

If you're finding yourself disliking how his brother treats him, or how he's gotten sucked into a family battle due to something that someone else said, you may have strong feelings about defending your partner, or about his willingness to get sucked into the family drama. The wisest thing for you both to do is not get drawn into the family battles as participants. Don't make that call or send that e-mail telling anyone off. Just ignore what you can, and support your spouse the best you can. He, too, might have a revolving family battle that always seems to go the same way.

To protect your marriage, insulate it from the emotional pain of your family's battles by telling each other that you're stressed or angry about something your sister said, and then don't repeat the story or at least not the long drawn-out sordid details beyond the basics. Tell your spouse that it's not a problem that can be solved, it's the same old thing, and that you don't want your bad mood right now to wreck the evening. Go take a bath, read a book, clean something, work on a craft, go for a walk, and let it fade. That's one way of handling it.

The other is to have a catchphrase between the two of you. If you would like your partner to defend you when your sister acts out toward you, just say to him "It's my sister." To which he'll respond, "She's just threatened by how beautiful and successful you are." That catchphrase will make you smile, knowing he has your back, and you've gotten the support you need to get through the same old battle. Without the damage to your relationship and without your partner criticizing you for having an old wound that just got smacked. It's a simple solution, and the storm clouds part much more quickly.

The First Time You Need to Ask Others for Help

It's never fun asking parents for money, but when disaster strikes and you need a temporary boost, the two of you need to support each other through the nerve-wracking process of asking for help, and support each other through the inevitable shame and disappointment that often follows *needing* some help. When it comes to asking for nonfinancial help, such as assistance with your move to a new house, the same feelings emerge. One or both of you might experience stress over what a parent or relative will think of you for not being able to handle this on your own. Perhaps a parent has been insensitive in the past and has made you or your partner feel inadequate. Those wounds will emerge again now. Now here's where newlyweds get tripped up: one thinks he can lighten the mood by making jokes. If you're deeply hurt and embarrassed by having to ask your parents for help, these jokes can come across as "you're not taking this seriously." Then you're in a big fight. When you're in this situation, you have to tell the other what you don't want to hear: "My father has shamed me in the past when I had to borrow money, so this is extremely hard for me. I know you're trying to help by joking, but I feel angry and alone when you do that. Just hug me and tell me it's all going to be okay." Your partner doesn't always know how deep your wounds are, or when he or she is touching them. You have to make it clear, and you'll get through this together.

Remind each other that asking for help is a sign of strength, even if it's hard to do. It takes great courage to go to anyone for assistance when you have a strong sense of pride and self-worth. Just remember, it's a sign of intelligence to know when it's wiser to ask for help than to allow things to fall apart further by avoiding solutions. Think about those who go bankrupt because they were too proud to ask for help. That hurts them and their family. If someone can help you, and you can repay them in kind, go for it as a way to protect your marriage and your future.

The First Time Others Ask You for Help That You Can't Give

As newlyweds, you may have limited funds for your own needs, so when a relative or friend comes to you for help with their money situation, it can be a very tough thing to say "no." What you may hear—and tons of newlyweds hear this even from their parents—is, "But you just got all that wedding money!" Clearly, this relative or friend thinks you're loaded, and they're counting on your good nature to help them out.

This is where newlyweds feel guilty, because so many friends and family just traveled so far to attend the wedding and were so generous with their gifts. The asker may be counting on that.

If you simply can't help them out with a financial gift and don't want the stress of waiting for a loan payback, and if your spouse has strong feelings that you have to say "no" to the asker, then the answer has to be "no." Just explain that the wedding money went to pay for the wedding, and that you'll both be recovering for a while. Offer to help in other ways if you can, but the wallet has to stay closed.

Will they be mad? Probably. They counted on your generosity— or on you caving in to pressure. Will they say mean things? Perhaps. But an important step in being newlyweds is to make these self-protective choices, even if you have to let someone down. This can be hard if you're the go-to guy or gal, the one everyone always counts on. Now, you're in a different place in your life, you may have a mortgage, you have big bills from the wedding and honeymoon, and you just can't hand out cash like you used to.

Life has changed, and change is always challenging. Others have to get used to the new you, and this new you will soon grow more confident. It won't be as hard next time. You just conquered the doormat syndrome together.

CHAPTER 13

Holiday Hassles

The holidays are supposed to be fun, right? Well, when you're newlyweds, you may just end up in a tug-of-war when each holiday rolls around. Who do you spend this year's Thanksgiving with? Most couples take turns between families, but that's a tough adjustment for all. In any given year, someone isn't getting to experience cherished family time and traditions. Read on to find out the best ways to adjust to new family responsibilities without dreading what's supposed to be a celebratory time.

The First Time You Divide the Holidays Between Both Parents' Places

If your sets of parents live nearby, you may be in the enviable position of being able to spend all holidays with both sets of parents. You'll go to one family earlier in the day, then travel to the other family later in the day. Even though this is a situation that many newlyweds wish they could enjoy, some conflict still creeps in there. How do you decide which family gets you "first?" How do you handle missing the dinner part of the festivities and only showing up for dessert? This is a scenario you both have to talk through carefully, since there are a lot of conditions present. For instance, your grandparents might not be at the dinner after 6 P.M. You don't want to miss seeing them.

The key here is flexibility. You might think it's wise to create a strict plan you'll use each year, alternating who gets you in the afternoon and who gets you after dinner, but life doesn't always divide that easily. So promise each other that you'll handle each year's shared holidays with true and fair flexibility, communicating any special circumstances, such as your sister's plans to be at your parents' house earlier in the day, so why don't you plan to take the early shift with your family this year? You have a long future ahead of you, and vowing now to flow with whatever's going on with relatives will take the stress out of your holidays.

There's also an option when parents live nearby for you to visit your in-laws for the first course, then you leave for your parents' place while your spouse stays with his family through the dinner meal, and then he comes to join you at your family's place for dessert. There's no rule that says you have to be joined at the hip, that you can only take one car! This fair and fun division plan allows you both to enjoy more time with your own families, then have together time with both groups. How does that work for you?

The First Time You Have to Take Turns Spending Holidays with Your Families

How do you figure *this* out? One of you is going to have to miss all or part of a family holiday, and that's one of the toughest issues facing all newlyweds. Your life has changed, and with it comes changes to your entire family circle. So if you're the one who has to give up Thanksgiving this year, don't mope through dinner at your in-laws. Give yourself permission to enjoy yourself, and see it as a gift to your spouse *and* your in-laws for you to be fully present and participating. You can, of course, steal away to a private room to call your family—they'll love that, and you'll feel better, too—so that you're present with them in some way as well.

Keep in mind that newlyweds and their parents do often create new holiday rituals, such as spending the day *before* Mother's Day taking one mom out to lunch, and the day of Mother's Day taking the other mom out to a lunch of her own, or they combine the families at one Mother's Day lunch served at their house. Problem solved.

In families where there are a lot of siblings and in-laws, it may be a norm that someone is missing from the table, so see this as your

AN UNEXPECTED PERK?

When the family misses you this year, next year's celebration will be all the more special. Perhaps the menu will include additional family favorite recipes or there will be a champagne toast. Most families deal with "on" and "off" years with married couples in the mix, so make each holiday special no matter where you are.

turn in the responsibilities of married life, and remind yourself that you wouldn't want to be an unloving partner by forcing your spouse to miss out on his or her turn at family gatherings.

The First Time You Try to Combine Family Traditions

You have nothing but good intentions, so when the holidays are at your place, you'll want to include traditions and dishes from both sides of the family. That can present some challenges, especially if dietary traditions are very different. Some families do not drink alcohol, while others have traditional drinks and toasts. This can be a tough battle, since it takes a gentle discussion of explaining to your in-laws that while you respect their beliefs, it wouldn't be fair or possible for you to change your family's traditions. Some newlyweds do decide to turn the dinner into a nonalcohol event, and then the teetotalers will leave with good tidings . . . right before the wine bottles are brought to the table. Compromise and respect are always key.

Overall, you'll find it's very easy and enjoyable to combine family traditions and dishes, and sharing these with everyone at your table really does cement the bonds between you. Be ready to explain the rituals to everyone so that no one feels left out or confused by what's going on.

You may encounter some resistance from relatives who don't want family traditions changed at all, but—and you probably learned this with your wedding—everyone's going to have to adjust. So there are two appetizers instead of the one your family expected. They'll get over it. Anyone who makes a fuss is just in their own drama. Just continue to enjoy hosting the holidays your way. And be sure to insert some of your own, new traditions as well, such as a dessert drink or some other new element that doesn't replace a longtime family ritual.

The First Conflict Over Religious Traditions

In most cases, you already have some experience with your spouse's religious rituals and traditions. Perhaps you've attended church together or enjoyed a Passover meal with the whole family . . . but now this is your married life, and you find that your spouse would like you to *really* observe their religious rituals, such as fasting or going to services. This is a topic that's ideally discussed before the wedding, but if you didn't get to it then, now's the time to discuss how you'd like your faiths celebrated. Be fair. If your spouse doesn't want to fast or abstain from eating meat on Fridays during Lent, you should never force him or her to do so. Don't even joke about your spouse not loving you enough.

Everyone is entitled to freedom of their religion. Some longtime marrieds find that they *eventually* drift into practicing each other's religious traditions, or they remain quite happily separate in their celebrations. Other couples find that they gravitate toward a new faith or spirituality together, over the years. So each of you should keep true to your own religious practices, be warm and inviting towards your spouse's curiosity to check them out, but lovingly accept it if it's just not for him or her. Your differences are an important part of marriage.

The First Conflict Over Buying Gifts for Family

The holidays often mean big shopping lists for loved ones' gifts, and conflicts can arise when one of you has always been far more generous to your family. With big bills from the wedding and your living expenses, it might be painful for you to see your spouse spending $600 on a Christmas gift for his niece. Does a four-year-old really need something that extravagant? Step back from this land mine. You both have your own spending money, and giving gifts to family is something that falls under your own domain. Would you feel right about giving a $20 gift to your niece now that you're married when you have always showered her with lovely presents?

On the other hand, as a married couple, your finances are a shared concern. And couples do remind each other that there is a mortgage to keep in mind. So work together to find less expensive but more sentimental gifts now that your shopping list has doubled in size. And if you're expected to buy separate gifts from *you* alone for his thirty relatives, stand your ground and suggest that you both sign the card for all the gifts that each of you will buy. Before your marriage, you may have felt fine giving little gifts to everyone on his side, but now it's a good solution for each of you to give a dual gift. Families understand and they'll switch to a dual gift for you next year. This is how you subtly insert a little change that works best for the two of you.

The First Fight About Holiday Travel

Who loves to travel during the holidays? Not too many people. Crowded airports. Flight delays. Hours sitting in traffic. Needing to take a day off of work to get to another state. This is one of those holiday stressors that is a universal condition for many families. So keep your stress levels lower by packing fun treats and soft drinks for the ride; bringing good reading material, earplugs, or an iPod for a flight filled with screaming kids; and keeping your sense of humor. This is a trip you have to take, and the getting there is the hardest part. The journey may not be too much fun, so don't complain and make it worse. And definitely don't pout or guilt-trip your spouse for dragging you away from your family this year. That's just going to drive a wedge between you.

Look at it as a wonderful adventure for the two of you, celebrate it as a first as newlyweds, and look forward to a warm, wonderful welcome when you arrive.

CHAPTER 14

In-Law Issues

There are probably five couples in the country who have no in-law issues. You're unlikely to ever find one on TV or in a movie. It's just a fact of life and a challenge for newlyweds, often right from the first minute you get home from the honeymoon. From meddling moms to bossy brothers-in-law, to really dysfunctional family patterns, these are your family members now . . . And like it or not, they'll be a part of your future. So now is the time for you to discuss how you'll handle in-law issues, or work on your *own* better mndset.

The First Conflict Over Interfering In-Laws

Some parents haven't gotten the memo that their son or daughter is an adult. They're just on automatic pilot with their advice and judgments, telling their kids what to do, and telling *you* what to do, either directly or through your spouse. Refrain from overreacting on this one. You're just at the first steps of their adjustment to your married life. Over time, they'll find that you or your spouse are not doing what they say, not acknowledging their usual manipulations, not putting your own lives on hold just to make them happy. It takes time, for them and for you. So look at this conflict as the start of a lifelong education in shifting toward a normal adult-adult relationship. You can say "no" to them without turning into a brat. You can thank them for their advice and then not follow it. Your spouse may need some time to transition to this new relationship. You really can't expect to change that overnight.

If your spouse isn't reacting to parents' interference, it usually means that he tunes it out. Don't get offended. This probably has nothing to do with you. It's just their family dynamic. You'll lead the way by very gently training the parent to accept that their "baby" isn't a baby.

❝A marriage counselor recently told me that the one thing newlyweds should never do is speak badly of or criticize their in-laws. She said it only hurts your spouse and creates resentment and conflict. I think it's probably the best advice I've ever gotten. Most people love their parents and hearing negative things about them can do damage to their relationship for years to come.❞

—Francesca Di Meglio, About.com Guide to Newlywed Life

And you're not subject to guilt trips. Again, it's going to be a long road, so practice good give-and-take, allow parents some things their way, and when major interference arises, master this line: "I can see how much you love (spouse), and your advice is coming from a place of love. That's always so nice to see. We'll keep your vacation idea in mind for a future trip, though. We're going to Hawaii this year." Or whatever sticking to your guns sounds like for you. Smile and be sweet. People come around much faster that way. And your spouse will so appreciate your avoiding a drama.

Personality Clashes with In-Laws

You're just not going to get along with everyone. If your in-laws really get under your skin, there may be fireworks. Or maybe the in-laws are just uptight, shy, standoffish, or have other quirks that are part of the package. You may really want to be embraced by your in-laws, but it's just not always going to happen the way, or with the speed, you want it to.

Some newlyweds find that the in-laws don't welcome them into the family at all. They're not addressed directly, or there are sighs and sneers when you speak. That just means the in-laws have issues they have to work on. You can't force your way into someone's heart, and you can't force a family to welcome you warmly like a daughter or son of their own.

The best course of action is to accept where you are with them right now, be cordial, peacefully coexist, be respectful, make efforts to connect, but allow them the right to take their time in getting to know and love you. Many newlyweds say this process took them *years*, but the in-laws eventually got the picture that you make their son or daughter happy.

If they want to be crabby, that's on them. Just continue to be your happy self, the blissful newlywed, and enjoy the warm welcome you're getting from other members of the family. Don't complain to your spouse about them not liking you. What can he do? He probably knows they're standoffish and uptight, and he's grown used to that.

The good news is that you're past working on the wedding with them, and now you're in the position of Deborah on *Everybody Loves Raymond*. Ray's parents consistently gave her a hard time, their personalities clashed, but a deep love grew over time, even though Ray's mother criticized Deborah's cooking and parenting skills incessantly. If you think of your in-laws like a sitcom family with their quirks, you can laugh off their comments before they turn to conflicts. They're just characters in your marriage.

In-Laws' Jealousy Over Time with Your Spouse

In-laws can get very needy and dependent on your spouse, especially if there's a pattern there already. If they were used to your spouse being available to them all the time, it's not so much fun for them to hear, "I have to check first" whenever they want to spend time with their son. There's jealousy there, and here's an important thing to keep in mind: *Parents are not always adults.* They may be in their 50s, 60s, or 70s, but

"If the in-laws are over at the house too often, invite them to come over for dinner every so often, perhaps once a month. Having a designated family night will show them that you care and want to be part of the family, but they can't come over all the time. Remember that your in-laws played a big role in creating the man or woman your spouse has become and for that you must show them respect and gratitude."
—Francesca Di Meglio, About.com Guide to Newlywed Life

emotionally they're about ten years old. The mistake so many newlyweds make is in giving their in-laws too much credit, and too much power. Your spouse might not have a Ph.D. in handling emotionally needy parents, but chances are he or she has some skills to deflect the demands. Trust in that deflection. If you look closer, you'll see that he is pretty good at brushing aside the endless requests for more together time with his parents. He's not going to say "no" 100% of the time, but you're getting your alone time together, too.

Over time, you'll find that you have the power to reduce some of that in-law jealousy, and your best move is to plan regular dinner nights or game nights, or brunches. Parents want to know they're not being abandoned, so when you give them a pattern to embrace, that gives them the security they need. Jealousy just means, "I'm afraid of losing you."

In-Laws Claiming Holiday and Vacation Time

Make it a rule that you won't make any holiday or vacation plans more than three months in advance. That sets a rule that most husbands say

WATCH OUT

The family might have an annual vacation they all look forward to, and you really can't step in and put an end to that. Talk with your spouse about how he or she feels about missing those weeks at the beach once in a while. Explain that you can't build your vacations around their trips, so how does every other year sound? Marriage is built on compromise.

they appreciate—it gives a boundary and allows you both to be more in control of planning your own downtime yet still gives you planning time for airfare and hotel room bookings! When parents hear your rule enough times, and when you stick to it, you're in the best position to plan your holidays and vacations fairly between the families and give yourselves the option of planning your own private getaways. A two- to three-month window lets you own your decisions and avoid way-in-advance grabs of your vacation time.

When in-laws go ahead and book a family vacation home a year in advance, figuring that it's easier to just do it rather than ask your permission, you may have to tell them "Sorry, but we already booked our summer vacation, and we don't have enough vacation days to take two trips this year." This is a hard confrontation to have, but it's essential for them to learn that they can't boss you around. Your spouse may want to give in this year, and you'll go along, but a gentle conversation will let them know that you are looking forward to a lifetime of family getaways and holidays, but to be fair, they really need to talk to you about them first. Don't say, "Ask me first," because you really can't establish yourself as the authority figure here. Be diplomatic in your phrasing—a sense of humor helps as well.

The First Mess-Up With the In-Laws

You really want your spouse's family to like you, but you just can't get to a point of comfort with them. They never really warmed up to you, and they seem to treat you like an outsider, especially if you didn't get the chance to establish a close relationship with them before the wedding. You never dreamed of having an adversarial relationship with your extended family, so you're trying extra hard to win them over.

And trying extra hard can lead to mistakes.

Let's say you invite his family over for dinner, envisioning a harmonious meal where everyone laughs and loves the food, only to find out that his mother is allergic to the seafood you cooked—you'll be stunned and upset that your effort failed. And worse, his mother seems to delight in knowing you're trying so hard to win her over. Some mothers-in-law are like that.

Pretty soon, you're crying into your pillow and your husband is trying to console you. Instead of lashing out at him for neglecting to tell you about the crab allergy, let him comfort you with plans to try it again another time. He knows his mom can be difficult, and he undoubtedly loves you for making the effort, even without a proper thank you from her.

The sad fact is, not all in-laws want to welcome a new son- or daughter-in-law into the family right away. It may take time and some power struggle. Repeated effort pays off, and in the meantime, you'll need to accept that you're in a holding pattern. And that trying a little less could pay off more.

Ask your spouse what will work best with her. Should you let her take the lead in conversations? Which topics should you talk about with her? Does she have any common interests with you? When you arm yourself with some talking points, you can turn the next family dinner into more of a success. Maybe slightly more, but it's a step in the right direction.

Don't expect to win her over right away. She may be a cranky woman who likes no one and enjoys criticizing others. And she doesn't want her son to like you better than her. She's going to be a challenge, a big one. So this first failure gives you a starting point. At least you tried.

Find it in your heart to forgive her for any rude comments as an investment in your marriage, because one of the foundations of a successful marriage is a peaceful coexistence with your spouse's family. (I know, it's a tall order when the mother in question really delivers some solid shots at you.) If you're clashing with them constantly, your spouse is going to feel so much pressure, caught in the middle. So let this first failure go and be optimistic about attempt number two. Tell your partner that you'd like to share a close relationship with his or her mother and that you'd like some guidance. He'll appreciate being asked, and he may give you some great keys, as in "She loves to talk about gardening." You can then bring a flower catalog to the next family party and point out the Queen of Sweden roses you thought she'd like to see. Baby steps . . .

Be assured, plenty of newlyweds have been in this position. Again, they've had to work really hard—including patience and pacing themselves—to earn the trust and love of extended family, and years down the road they laugh about their first nervous meetings. Many parents say quite honestly that they weren't aware that you were so nervous, or that they hated having to tell you they were allergic to the crab. They want to be liked as much as you do, so during the first year of marriage keep in the forefront of your mind that your deep desire to create a happy marriage means that everything will seem a little more intense to you right now. It is for everyone.

First Fight Over a Loyalty Decision

This conflict is one in which you might share part of the blame. Don't expect that just because you're married your spouse will always take your side, put your wishes before his family's wishes, or put your plans before his parents' plans for you. In many instances, you're setting yourself up for conflict by testing your spouse's loyalty. *Will he choose me over them?* There's a huge flaw in that kind of thinking. You can't have a happy marriage if you—yes, you—set up an adversarial, competitive situation that puts your spouse in the hot seat. He does have longtime loyalty to his family, which doesn't take away from his loyalty to you. Everyone has to share and compromise throughout the marriage.

That might be a tall order if his or her family is setting up the loyalty tests—which many newlyweds experience. His mom might be the one setting your partner up with demands that conflict with plans he already has with you. So here's a script to avoid loyalty gaffes: "I'm not going to make you choose between me and your family, but in instances where we already have plans, I really don't want you to ditch your promises to me to make your mother happy. That's not fair, and you wouldn't like it if I did the same. When she asks you to commit to a plan, would you please just tell her that we have something going on that day?" Or "I felt like you threw me under the bus at lunch, and while I know that wasn't your intention, I'd just like you to avoid joking about my views in front of your family."

The First Criticism of What You're Doing

Why are you marinating the steaks in that *sauce?* When your spouse questions how you're doing something that seems simple to you, it can feel like a kick to the stomach. At no time do we want to be parented by our spouses, so an out-of-left-field criticism is going to kick up any issue you have with *criticism* itself. And then, if you're not careful, you're snapping at your spouse and an argument is underway . . . especially if you overreact with the classic, "You're *always* telling me what to do!" In newlywed weeks and months, you may be a little oversensitive, taking any criticism as a rejection. And that goes double when the criticism comes from in-laws, because that perceived rejection really stings. You already thought they didn't think highly of you, and now this is proof, right?

So make a note, and keep it in mind, that not everything is a criticism, or a judgment of your abilities. It may be just one of those thoughts that comes out without filtering (and come on, admit it, you've done the same thing to your partner!). It really could be that your spouse or sister-in-law just wants to know why you're using that sauce, because you *are* such a great cook, and he or she is trying to learn from you. It could actually be a positive comment.

So let that first criticism go, or meet it with a humorous reply, such as "We were out of mayonnaise and beer." When you're less defensive, the criticism becomes just a statement. If your partner is criticizing too much, though, and you feel he or she wants you to change too often, that's the time for a serious request of "Please don't tell me how to make dinner. We'll use your sauce next time." Over time, you'll coexist and accept how the other does things. These little critiques are just the learning path to get there. As for critiquing in-laws? Just shake it off as many times as it takes for them to figure out they can't rattle you.

Many in-laws have said that a daughter- or son-in-law who could take their ribbing and zing them right back earned their respect. "I don't like people who take themselves too seriously," says one father-in-law. Think of the movie *The Family Stone*. Once Meredith lightened up a little, she was "in" with the family. (Just don't go out and get drunk with his brother to do so, as happened in the movie!)

The First Conflict Over Inequitable Holiday Sharing

Parents are shrewd. They know how to guilt you into plans for Easter, Thanksgiving, and Christmas, and they can often forget about the task

HOW OLD ARE YOU?

Some parents aren't mature and they want to "win" you and your spouse. If they can get you to spend the holidays with them, then they've "beaten" the other family. Sad, but true, and many newlyweds who are themselves emotionally mature get stuck with a baffling tug-of-war in the form of early and guilt-infused invitations. Once you understand that the matter is more about competition, you can tame the game by saying a simple, "We were with you last year. Now it's my partner's family's turn. Thanks for inviting us, though. We'll look forward to your turkey next year—it's always so delicious." And victory will be yours!

of sharing you with the in-laws. So you both have to make it a solemn vow that you'll divide holidays equally, even if it means traveling to where your families live.

The first time you clash over an unfair plan to spend yet another holiday with either of your families, you could end up with a lot of sadness in your own emotional well—you don't want to miss out on your family traditions. And one of you has to.

This is one of those things that's going to take some getting used to, and the argument is just the sadness venting. It's also one of those great arguments for newlyweds to have, because you'll remember to be extra careful about dividing holidays equally in the future. Would you or your partner put as much effort into equal time if you *hadn't* just had a blowup over it? Perhaps not.

Just steer clear of accusing your partner of favoring one family over the other, don't drag in family problems or issues that need to be handled with diplomacy, like his annoying sister or her grandmother's bad cooking. That's just going to cause bigger problems. Every family has a strange person, a troubled person, a bad bean dip, but these personalities and issues should not be used as weapons against your spouse when you're trying to "win" the holidays at your family's place. For better or for worse, as you agreed, the holidays should be split evenly.

In-Laws Who Ask Inappropriate Questions

Some people don't know what an inappropriate question is. That's why you may get so many "When are you going to have a baby?" inquiries starting just a few hours after you exchange wedding vows (see pages 233–234 for more on this gem). Just smile and thank the person for caring (give them the benefit of the doubt) and deliver your stock answer: "We'll get back to you when the time is right." Newlyweds should arm themselves with a collection of vague but polite comebacks to a range of inappropriate questions, which can include:

- "So, is the thrill gone yet?"
- "How's the ol' ball and chain?"
- "How much did the wedding cost?"
- "How much did your house cost?"
- "You've gained *how much* weight since the wedding? Gosh, you were so thin that day!"
- "Is it 50% of marriages that end in divorce these days?"
- "So, is your sex life dead yet?"

As you can see, all inappropriate questions originate from a person's inability to make proper conversation or from a poor sense of humor. People who are jaded about marriage in general seem to be the worst offenders. You don't have to "be nice" and answer these questions, because they're usually not questions that are asked to be answered. They're just the asker's way of showing everyone he or she has issues.

Newlyweds can amuse themselves by coming up with their own funny responses to these oddball questions, some you can use in polite company and some you can't. And even if you're short on witty comebacks, a simple, "No comment" gets right to the point.

When Your Family Gets Your Spouse Upset

Regardless of whether or not they mean to, a member of your family has hurt your spouse by something they have said or done. That puts you in an important yet difficult position. You have to comfort your spouse. No question about it. *Don't* insult him or her by saying, "Oh, that's just how they are" or "Don't be so sensitive." That's a serious injury to an already injured spouse. Hug, kiss, comfort, give a foot rub to provide immediate loving care, then tell your spouse you'll talk to the offender. That's loyalty in action.

Ideally, your spouse will take the initiative to stand up for herself or himself when your parents or siblings act harshly, but that's not always a natural reaction in the first few months of marriage when your partner doesn't yet have the comfort level to say "Hey, knock it off!" He or she is probably in a stage of wanting to be proper and respectful, and when those hurtful comments occur, your spouse is more apt to freeze than to fire right back at them. In time, they will have enough depth to the relationship to handle all interpersonal issues directly. Right now, though, you *can't* let your good-natured spouse get pummeled by your family. It's time for an action to remedy the problem at the source. You'll then need to talk with your parents or siblings and say, "Hey, that comment you made to (spouse) the other day was really hurtful and rude. I'd like you to apologize." When that person balks and says your spouse is being silly, the only correct answer is, "That may be how you see it, but my spouse is very important to me, and I don't want any animosity between the two of you. I think it was rude, so please either call or e-mail an apology right away. I'm serious." You have to take a stand, because you'll lose your spouse if you stand back and allow him or her to be bullied, judged, teased, insulted, or hurt by your family members. It's time to take an adult stand with your family, even if it's a tough conversation.

CHAPTER 15

Fears of the Future

You promised to love and cherish for all time, and your vows talked about sharing a beautiful future together, but now with the wedding buzz and your honeymoon tan fading, it hits you: There's a *lot* that can happen in the future. Some newlyweds flip out, worried about money or their jobs or how they'll provide for a family someday, and it can be terrifying. *This is adult life.* They panic. Suddenly, "I'm a wife" becomes "*Uh, oh,* I'm a wife."

It's completely normal to have anxieties about the future. Have you seen the self-help section of the bookstore lately? It's filled with books on how to face an uncertain future. Do you know anyone who's not worried about something in the future? Retirement? Having kids? Buying a house? Their career? It's a part of human nature, but that doesn't make it any less scary for you. Here are some ways to face future fears together and keep them from chipping away at the foundation of your marriage.

The First Time You're Asked "When Are You Having Kids?"

Some couples hear it at their wedding: "So when are you two going to have a baby?" *What? Can I finish eating my slice of wedding cake first?*

Now there's a very important element to this challenge: What's your stress level right now? If you're feeling pressured over many things—as you will be during the planning of a wedding, and also during the adjustment to married life—you may feel that this is one more big thing thrown on your plate that you're not looking for. The person asking the question probably didn't mean any harm or pressure, but that's how it usually feels. You may take it as someone rushing you into the next big thing. So you might get very angry over something more than the question itself. It becomes a matter of rushing you; of trying to control the pace and timing of your life. And it's personal.

If you've already had these feelings about a parent or in-law, then the stress gets magnified.

Again, they're most likely just wishing something that they think is *good* for you, a blessing. Maybe they have it in their hearts that you're such a great couple, so loving and so compassionate, that you'll be terrific parents. And maybe that's just something they say at weddings. It might not have any intended wallop at all. But that's not necessarily how you take it. So you and your new husband may clash over it, if you're not in tune with the preparations you can take to handle this challenge.

Allow the wave of pressure to wash over you, not stick to you, not spike your blood pressure or make your blood boil. Remove the harm from the sentence and *choose* to take it as a positive wish. A poorly timed one, but a positive wish. With the venom removed, you can now handle this challenging First with the following responses:

- "Wow, we haven't even begun to think about expanding our family. But thank you for the good wishes." That's it. Done. You've done what savvy politicians do, and you smoothed over the question. Good job.
- "Not anytime soon. We plan to enjoy the next few years together before we even think about having a baby." And change the subject to a compliment about what the asker is wearing, or something about *them* to move away from the baby issue.
- "When we get to that point, we'll let you know."
- One of my favorites: "(Spouse) is going to be an amazing parent someday. I'm so lucky to have him. Maybe in five or six years when we accomplish our marriage goals first, then we'll start talking about kids."

What you should *not* do is get defensive. This topic came up on one of my Q&A message boards recently, and someone suggested a rather snotty answer to the effect of "When we decide to have unprotected sex, we'll let you know." There's no need for that. You just come off as an angry person, and your response to their innocent question would be an unwarranted attack. So think about what your calm responses would be, and share them with your groom, because well-meaning relatives are going to ask him, too.

Now what happens if you have decided that you don't want to have children? You've discussed your future plans seriously between the two of you, and that—for now—is how it should stand: just between the two of you. Especially when you're just home from the honeymoon, you may be asked by many well-meaning friends and relatives about when you plan to start a family, and you're best-served by telling them—quite honestly—"We're not even thinking about that now." So true. For the sake of peace, avoid divulging your decision not to have children, because you'll most likely be met with a shocked *"What? How could you say that?"* or other offensive comment that's only going to stress you out. It's no one's business right now, and it's a surefire challenge to your new marriage if parents mount a campaign to change your minds. It's far better to just remove the topic of kids until you're good and ready to share your decision with others.

Bottom line: Don't turn this first into an unnecessary conflict by letting your emotions and current frustrations get the best of you. You may be asked this question many times over the next few months and years, so collect an arsenal of responses that elevate you both.

Your Future Financial Goals

Who *doesn't* have financial fears right now? Especially if you've paid for all or part of your wedding, or recently bought a home or a new car. Your credit cards might be screaming right now, your wallet aching, and your net worth not quite where you'd like it to be. The only way to handle financial fears is to create a plan for reducing debt, saving, and changing your lifestyle with smarter financial decisions as the centerpiece. Being in good shape financially produces a healthier state of mind and a sense of security, while debt drains your energy, and puts your future financial goals farther from your reach. So sit down and make your wise money plans, face those hard numbers (like the balances on your credit cards), and make it a team effort to educate yourselves on the basics of smarter financial health. Get a financial advisor as a wise investment in helping you reach your goals, and reward yourselves for good behavior (just not with a spending spree!).

Most importantly, remain optimistic that you will dig out of debt, you will have abundance, and you'll have a great life in the future due to the financial security you're building right now.

Once you've cleared the hurdle of the first argument over your financial goals, the door is open for you both to communicate about your financial worries, forgive each other for financial missteps, like going above the budget to get a new power tool or some ultrapricey towels. Again, you'll have triumphs and challenges when facing your financial lifestyle rules, but you're in this together, for richer or for poorer. Money is a *very* emotionally loaded topic, so proceed with care.

Find a great financial advisor who can help you reach your financial goals, and who can answer your tax and investment questions.
Don't just pick a name in the phone book. Ask relatives, friends, and colleagues who they work with and trust. Word of mouth is the best way to find a financial professional candidate to research and interview.

WORK ON YOUR CREDIT

Start setting the foundation for your dream home by paying down your debts and building a better credit rating. That's a key element to being able to afford a home down payment and mortgage.

Your Future Home Goals

Shake off those fears about never being able to afford a house of your own. If you work to improve your credit rating, partner on saving up, and read everything you can on home purchasing, you're doing your part to work toward that dream home. It might not be a mansion on the California coast, though. It is important to be realistic about the fact that you'll probably begin with a smaller home, then upgrade as time goes on. Most longtime-married couples remember fondly when they were in their starter homes—how small it was, how noisy the neighbors were, but how much love they filled it with. So enjoy what's within your reach, make no decisions impulsively out of fear, and know that good luck can arrive at any time with an affordable home in a great neighborhood, small and ready to be filled with love. And then the next one will appear years from now.

Fears About Health Issues

One or both of you might have some health issues right now, or you may have observed a friend or family member whose health created a big challenge for their life and relationships. Rather than be paralyzed by fear, be proactive by going for regular checkups, seeing a doctor right away if you have any health concerns, eating healthy, avoiding bad habits, and getting plenty of exercise. As newlyweds, this is the perfect time to establish a healthier lifestyle, value your health for the sake of your partner as well as yourself, and put those fears to rest with every clean bill of health.

If you do face a health crisis at any time in the future, know that just about every type of medical condition has an association that offers educational literature, free counseling and support for the patient and caregivers, and there's often financial help available and contact with survivors and volunteers who can help you through any tough time. When one person is sick, the entire family is affected by the illness, so you all must practice the best self-care possible. We're lucky to live in a time with such great resources and readily available information, new studies, and powerful medicines. That can ease your health fears tremendously, as can looking around at all the family and friends in your life. They'll be there for you, too.

An Unplanned Pregnancy

But we're not ready to have a baby yet! When it's *that* fear that strikes, many a newlywed has broken out into a cold sweat. Sure, an unplanned pregnancy might not be a trauma for you, but there may be a fair amount of panic about your finances, careers, your home, your lifestyles. You may just not be at that point yet!

Newlyweds who have had pregnancy scares say that the biggest challenge was a spouse who shut down emotionally, who was distant, and who avoided the topic rather than support the other spouse. Don't let that happen to you. Because if you learn that it was a false alarm, the feeling that remains is that one of you abandoned the other in a time of need.

It's important for the two of you to talk about when it will be time for a baby, if you choose to have one, but it's equally important for you to talk about how you'll handle it if that news comes sooner than you'd like. Perhaps this pregnancy scare was a good thing. It got you to think about creating an emergency fund, or you discussed which of you would stay home with the baby, or you both found out your companies' family leave policies. Challenges are there to get you talking, planning, preparing, and learning, and you also learn a great deal more about your partner during any scare. How will you measure up during a pregnancy scare? Will you draw closer to your partner, or will your actions leave a scar that will last forever?

Your First Conflict Over Family Planning

If one of you is ready to have a baby and the other spouse wants to wait, you may find yourselves locked in a very emotional conflict. You may think your partner is keeping you from something you want badly. Before this conflict becomes insurmountable, bear in mind that couples have separated over biological clock conflicts, and you don't want that to happen. Handle the issue in a methodical way: Each of you should write down why now is and isn't the time to start trying to conceive. When you see your spouse's "no" list containing the entry: 1) We're $20,000 in debt from school loans and the wedding—we wouldn't have enough extra money to give the child great things now, your "yes" reason

#1 of "I always said I'd have a baby before age thirty" pales in comparison. Talk it out without trying to convince your partner to change his or her mind. Right now, you're just working to fully understand his or her hesitancy. It wouldn't be fair to the baby if one partner wasn't ready yet. And forget friend's advice to "Just do it! Your spouse will come around." That's trouble on the horizon. Don't try to set a date for trying to conceive, because who can tell what the future will bring? Just set the topic aside without anger towards your spouse; hone your parenting skills with nieces, nephews, and friends' kids; and look forward to the conflict-free day when you're both ready to start a family. Your spouse has a right to say no now, as do you, and it wouldn't be kind, loving, or fair to pressure him or her.

Fears About Work Issues

You both might have work anxiety. Most people do, especially during times when layoffs are a possibility, or if you simply dislike your job. Now, with the financial challenges of starting a new life together, you might *really* be feeling the pressure to perform at work, make more money, and keep your job. Some people lie awake at night worrying about losing their livelihoods.

As newlyweds, you'll support each other and provide the encouragement and validation that neither of you is getting from your managers or bosses. You'll soothe hurt feelings when a jealous coworker snipes or steals an idea. You'll keep an eye on job postings for each other's new job search, and review each other's resumes, perhaps suggest ideas for each other's big projects. The wonderful thing about having a partner is that you get a fresh, new perspective on your work environment and projects. You're often too close to the job to see the positives, and your partner's viewpoint could make you feel better about where you are and give you the boost to improve your own morale or resume-strength. Maybe you'll suggest some higher education to your partner, share a great business book or an article online, and connect your partner to your friends, family, and colleagues so that he or she can network in a big way.

This big challenge to newlywed couples is a fact of life for most people, but as a team, you can overcome work fears together. You might even find that you're drifting toward an entirely new line of work introduced by your spouse or by a friend you just met at the wedding. Is there room at your spouse's uncle's firm? You might just be in a great position to take a step up in the world.

Fears About Marriage in General

It never fails. Someone makes the comment about 50% of all marriages ending in divorce, and your alarm bells go off. Perhaps your parents were unhappily married, or maybe you have a divorce behind you yourself. Fears about marriage can make a marriage hard to navigate, so you have to do the personal work required to face these worries, share your fears with your partner, and invest your time and focus on acquiring the skills to *be* a great marriage partner. You do have some say in how your marriage will turn out. No matter what your miserable mother or bitter friends say about lifelong commitments.

Think of it this way: When you first started on your wedding plans, it was probably very overwhelming. A wedding is a giant thing, right? A big mass of responsibilities and to-dos and things possibly going wrong and people possibly saying something wrong . . . and you spun yourself out of control because it was just too big of an issue. But once you started breaking it down into bite-sized chunks, like "call the florist with our flower list" and "choose a wedding cake," you found it to be far less intimidating with your focus on one task at a time. One meeting with a caterer. One fax to your photographer to deliver your itinerary. It's the same with marriage. It might not be cakes and flowers, but rather "paying bills," "time with in-laws," "having date nights," "time for sex," and "grocery shopping." You can handle each one of those things, just like it was a snap to fax in your list to the photographer.

A marriage is a big commitment *and* a lot of work, especially at this early stage when you're adjusting to a new life with each other. So talk about what you want each "chapter" of your marriage to be like. How do you want to spend vacations someday? How do you prefer to share tasks? When you delve into the sections of your marriage, you'll find that you're cocreating a great life together, even if you make some mistakes along the way.

And you will. So make apologizing part of your arsenal for a long and happy marriage. Success is built on the dust of mistakes and apologies. And when fears about marriage arise, remind yourself of all that's great about your spouse and your partnership and how lucky you are to have each other. Make a list if you have to. If friends are having troubles in their marriages, observe what they're doing and don't make

"It's important not to fear your parents' marriage models—they were developed by different people than you and your spouse, in a different time, for different reasons. Besides, you probably didn't see your parents as newlyweds or when they were just courting. By all means, think about your parents' models, use them for discussions, but don't be too critical about your spouse's parents. Don't say 'Your dad never helped at home.' Say, 'I know your parents didn't share child care, but I think we're a little different, and I'd like you to be as involved with the kids as I am.'"
—Tina Tessina, Ph.D., Author of *Money, Sex, and Kids*

the same mistakes. You can see it when one of them is disrespecting the other, breaking confidences and talking down to the other. Learn from what you see going on around you.

And if you argue, don't be afraid. Arguing is a good thing in marriage. That's where the useful information comes out in the steam of an outburst. It's where you get your best lessons. Then you make up, and each other's needs are clearer.

"But we never had a fight" is one of the most common statements made by divorcing couples. They weren't close enough to be honest with each other.

The First Time You Think "Maybe We Did the Wrong Thing"

Cold feet don't just happen before the wedding. Many newlyweds say they had moments, or days, when they feared they made a mistake in marrying their partners. It comes on like a flu bug, making you queasy and weak, and permeates your thinking. *Is this the person I'm supposed to be with?*

When your question is, "Was it right to get married?" your best course of action is to make a list of all the ways it is definitely right, all of the things your partner does well, the strength of your commitment to your partner, the fun you have, the warm feeling you get when you hear that key in the door. Then do some journaling about what your life would be like if you were to leave today. What would you miss about your partner, about your home? Would you miss your in-laws? Family holidays?

If thinking about life without your partner makes you feel relieved, then you should get to a counselor to talk out what you need in your life that you're not getting, how you might be able to get it from your marriage, if it's time for couples' counseling, or if you really should leave. And abuse is not to be tolerated, even if you would miss your home and your in-laws.

Your First Doubts About Your Partner

After the wedding, the bubble bursts. You or your partner may have relaxed your standards, started caring less about how you treat each other, how you dress, or your manners. Before the wedding, you may have had an idealized view of your spouse. With all of those romantic dinners and fun engagement parties, you saw your spouse as the best person on earth. You didn't see all of his or her flaws. But now that the wedding buzz has worn off, those flaws are staring you in the face. Mr. Wonderful never changes the toilet paper roll and tells dumb jokes at dinner parties. He doesn't wear deodorant on the weekends. And he's looking at you with your hair in a ponytail, listening to you complain to your friends on the phone, noticing that you haven't shaved your legs in days. Welcome to marriage, where everything gets very *real*.

These little details that are all so clear now can cause you doubts about your partner. Did he present a better-than-usual image just to get you down the aisle? Was he always such a slob? He might think, "Was she always this needy?"

As a newlywed, you have to take the bad with the good. No one is "on" 100% of the time, and it's an unkindness to expect them to be. Forgive the unshaven days and the cranky moods, and he'll forgive your stubble and your overuse of curry in everything you cook. Newlyweds learn to use humor expertly: "Bring that long toenail over here. I have to punch a hole in this can of juice." That said with a hug gets your partner laughing with you, but he'll soon be clipping that talon. Only you know your partner's tolerance for jokes. You know what motivates him or her best.

And you know when you're making too big a deal out of a "human moment" or a bad day that everyone gets to have while in the comfort of a loving relationship. But if he still won't use deodorant, just tell him that he gets no sex until he does.

The First Time Someone Hits on You . . . and You're Tempted

Just don't do it. Nothing is worth hurting your spouse, your families, your friends, and *you* if you take the bait. Some people actually pursue married men and women as a sport, just to see if they can "win" someone away from their wedding vows and "beat" the spouse. Anyone who would do so is a snake with no sense of decency. It's someone who will hurt anyone to get what they want in the moment. And they don't even value the thing they're pursuing (that would be you). That'll get you to look at that flirty coworker differently. Not so hot now, is he?

The First Time You Recognize a Bad Relationship Pattern in Yourself

It's extremely hard to admit when you're doing something wrong. Most often, you're not even aware that you're doing it in the first place. But when your spouse tells you—in an argument or in a loving conversation—that you're being demanding or guilt-trippy or inconsiderate, a very unwelcome lightbulb will go off in your head . . . *He's right.*

Maybe it's a friend or a parent or an in-law or coworker who loves you enough to point out your missteps, but the message is the same: You're doing a relationship don't. Ouch.

Your first step is going to be an apology to your spouse. "I truly didn't recognize that I was giving you a guilt trip by talking about the vacation I wished we were planning. I see your point, and I'm very sorry." You could say "It won't happen again," but you know what? It probably will. We're all big masses of unconscious behavior, and we repeat things many times before we get them right. So prevent a fresh fight about this by saying, "Would you please point it out to me if I do this again?" What a great gift to your spouse! You're showing that you truly care about changing your pattern, you're trusting your partner to remind you, and you're working to correct your own mistake in the relationship.

You might make this a fun thing, by telling your spouse that he gets a foot rub whenever you slip up. There's a motivator for you!

Work on your relationship mistakes, take an honest look at how well you're adhering to the Golden Rule, ask yourself how you'd feel if *he* guilt-tripped you about everything or acted jealous every time you went out with the girls. You're at the start of a long learning journey together, and you'll *both* unravel your unconscious relationship mistakes during this ride of your marriage. What matters most is that you always keep trying to get it right.

The First Friends of Yours Who Divorce

It's one of those stunning phone calls you never forget: A friend of yours, whose wedding you attended, is getting divorced. Maybe someone cheated, maybe they've been unhappy for years. These are your *friends*, and their marriage didn't last.

Depending on how big a deal divorce is to you (some people are more shaken by it than others), this can be a trying time for your marriage. *If this can happen to them . . .*

Other people's realities will come crashing into your marriage, and you might be drawn into their drama. Which friend in the couple do you stay close to? Whom do you invite to dinner parties? Maybe you're hearing the sordid details as a friend and confidante. A side effect: their divorce is making you nervous in your own marriage. *If this can happen to them . . .*

Rule number one about friends' divorces: You never know the whole story. No one does. Probably not even the *couple*. So don't take their divorce drama, diagnose them, and inspect your marriage for signs of the same. *He's coming home a half hour late from work!* You're not a top-notch detective, and you're not a psychologist or a marriage counselor. Your friends simply couldn't make it work.

You don't know how hard they tried, if they were honest with each other, if there was an outside influence. All you can know at any time is what is true for yourself. *How dedicated am I to my own marriage?*

Maybe this divorce in your circle of friends is a good wake-up call for the two of you.

Maybe it's time to show your affection to your spouse a little more, appreciate the things he or she does, plan more dates, ask about her day, give him more time to himself on the weekends, surprise her with a thoughtful little gift, reminisce about your first date, send an e-mail just to say hello in the middle of the day. Act like you're in the beginning stage of dating. Cleanse any injuries or resentments that you can feel sitting there between you. Apologize if you have to for something you said the other day. Let him off the hook for weekend plans you forced on him and promise more notice next time. Don't screen his mother's phone calls. A great marriage takes work, understanding, and compromise, and this divorce can remind you to appreciate your partner more.

The First Time You Consult an Expert for Marriage Help

Repeat these words out loud: It's a sign of strength to ask for help.

A good relationship counselor knows just how to clear the path of debris so that you can communicate with each other, and you'll get useful tasks designed to bring you closer to one another. The key is a *good* relationship counselor, so invest the time to find a great one who meshes with your personalities. You might need to visit four or five before you find the right one, and then you'll proceed in the process with full focus on fixing what's wrong in your marriage, as well as within yourself. Because marriage problems are never one person's fault. It takes two to create and solve problems.

WHEN TO LOOK FOR A THERAPIST

Here are some points from the section "Guidelines for Finding and Using Therapy Wisely" in *Money, Sex, and Kids*:

* You have problems, either as individuals or as a couple, that you can't solve by yourself or by talking to friends and family.
* You cannot control such behaviors as temper tantrums, alcohol or drug addiction, painful relationships, anxiety attacks, or depression.
* You have serious difficulties communicating in your relationships.
* You have sexual problems or sexual dysfunction that does not go away by itself.
* You or your partner become verbally or physically abusive (even once).
* One or both of you have a general, pervasive unhappiness with your life.
* You and your partner have disagreements and struggles you can't resolve yourselves.
* Your partner keeps telling you something's wrong with your relationship, but you don't believe it's true (or you're trying to tell your partner there's a problem and he or she won't listen).

"When we first decided to get married, my husband and I made a deal that we'd go for counseling for any problem we couldn't solve by ourselves in three days. That rule has served us well for twenty-five years. In our first years, we went a few times, which helped us avoid creating dysfunctional patterns, and taught us how to work together. Because we went when the problems were small, they never got too big. We haven't needed a session in years, but if one of us says 'I think we need to go for counseling,' it's enough of an indication of dissatisfaction that the other spouse gets right down to problem-solving.

If your partner won't go for counseling, don't forget you can do it by yourself. That's usually the most powerful way to motivate a reluctant partner."

—Tina Tessina, Ph.D., Author of *Money, Sex, and Kids*

As newlyweds, you're in the best position of your entire lives together to create a great foundation right now, address problems before they grow, protect your partnership, make each other feel loved and secure, and make your marriage fun and romantic. You're going to be that couple on the beach, withered and gray and stooped, still holding hands, still lighting up when you see each other across the room. It *is* possible. Now is when you plant the seeds for it.

NOTE FROM THE AUTHOR

You are now a couple who knows how to make the most of your first year of marriage, especially those first few, glowing weeks when you're freshly home from the honeymoon. You won't let all the big and little moments of celebration pass you by while you're blinded by work tasks and housekeeping. You won't switch into autopilot now that the wedding's over . . . which is when *other* couples experience postwedding blues.

You're not going to be that couple who gets disillusioned by marriage, because you're keeping an eye out for the best parts of your partnership and turning them into a party. And you're also looking out for the most common challenges that newlyweds face, so that you're not blindsided by them. You have the tools to face them now, so that you can still be the radiant recent bride and the dashing handsome groom for months after the big day. Who wouldn't want to extend the magic of being newlyweds?

I wish you much luck and every blessing in your new life together, and I welcome your stories for future editions of this book. Write to me at www.sharonnaylor.net with your stories of how the ideas in this book helped you, and suggest your own ideas for *Home from the Honeymoon* celebrations. I'd love to hear from you.

All the best,

Sharon Naylor

Our Journal Pages

Our Journal Pages

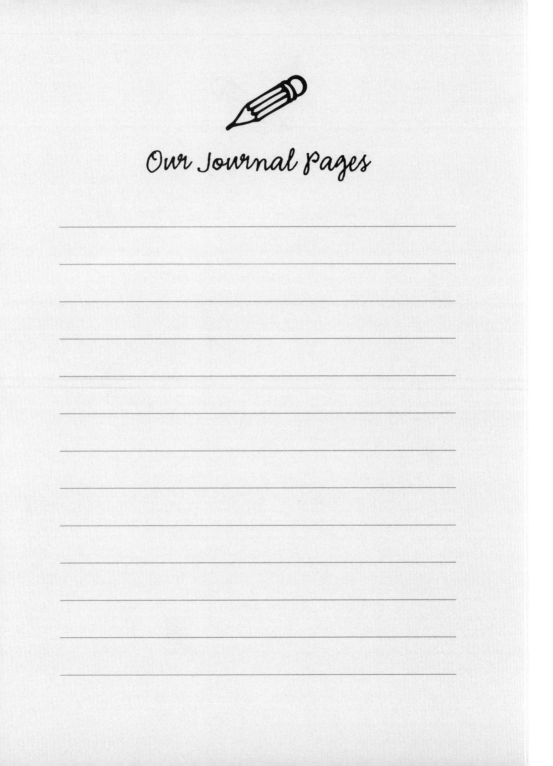

Our Journal Pages

Our Journal Pages

Our Journal Pages

_____

_____

_____

_____

_____

_____

_____

_____

_____

_____

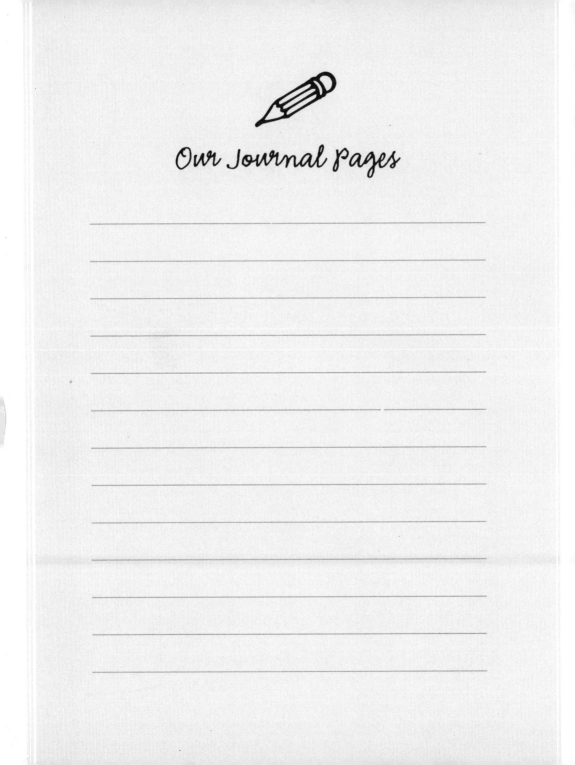

Our Journal Pages